WHAT THEY ARE ABOUT #MOMLIFE

"#MOMLIFE is like a needed ray of sunshine and a breath of fresh air for moms seeking encouragement in the Word as we raise children for Christ. Alison's authenticity, joy, wisdom, and passion to minister to mothers and families comes through every page, bringing hope and joy to all. I highly recommend this book for every mom, young and old."

Rebecca Keener, author of The Marvelous Madness of Motherhood and host of Always More TV

"Alison Wallwork has written an outstanding book that will encourage you in your parenting journey! As you read #MOMLIFE, you'll find faith-filled encouragement, scriptures to grab onto, and laugh at her real, down-to-earth stories as she shares from her heart."

Beth Jones, pastor and author, Kalamazoo, MI

"#MOMLIFE devotionals are refreshing, resourceful, and real. Each chapter focuses on the healing power of God's grace on us mamas and allows us to fall at His feet with our challenges and struggles. A great reminder that He does not give us more than we can handle, these daily devotions are filled with hope, joy, grace, and mentorship. Reading through the chapters could easily be the best spent five minutes of your day."

April Walker, Connected Families Ministry Team, Eden Prairie, MN

#MOMLIFE

A 16-week devotional study for moms

Alison Wallwork

Sarah,
I love YOU so much and thank Jesus for our sweet friendship. I hope you had a wonderful birthday! This mommy devotional is amazing! I hope it (He) speaks to your heart, as it has for me.

♡ always
Jia
XOX (2019)

#MOMLIFE

DEVOTIONAL STUDY

ALISON WALLWORK

#MOMLIFE Devotional Study
by Alison Wallwork

Edited by: Adam Colwell, Adam Colwell's WriteWorks, LLC
Cover design by:
Typesetting by:
Published by:

Printed in the United States of America
ISBN (Paperback): 978-0-578-40805-7

I dedicate this devotional to the four wild and wonderful boys that have made me a mom. Your uncanny knack for calling my name the second I walk into the bathroom has always ~~irritated~~ amazed me (you know I'm smiling). Thank you for providing lots of material for me to use! Through parenting you, I've come to better understand the heart of God as my Heavenly Father, and for that, I'm so grateful. Keep shining bright, my loves.

ACKNOWLEDGMENTS

To my amazing husband, Aryan, thank you for believing in me. Thank you for loving me and for pursuing my heart. God gave me more than I ever dared hope for when He gave me you, and I'm eternally grateful.

To Malaki, Zayne, Mataio, and Jase, I am grateful every day for the privilege of being your mom! Thank you for keeping our lives exciting and full of life, love, and material to write about! My prayer is that you will catch onto God's love and purpose for you and pursue Him relentlessly.

To my mom, who lost her battle with cancer and left our lives way too soon, thank you for always praying for me through the years, and for all your hard work as a single mom. I totally get it now why you would go into the bathroom, lock the door, and not let me talk to you through the crack underneath! I miss you every day.

To my mother-in-law, thank you for the many times you watched the boys and folded our laundry so that I could write. I'm not sure where I'd be on this journey of motherhood without your continued love, prayers, and help along the way. Thank you for raising such an incredible man that I get to do life with!

To Adam, my writing coach and editor, I truly appreciate the way you've challenged me to grow as a writer. You've been wonderful to work with, and I look forward to future projects together.

To the spiritual mamas who have poured God's love and truth into my life along the way, thank you! You've encouraged and challenged me to keep going, to breathe, and to trust God. I'm thankful for your wisdom, mentorship, and support.

CONTENTS

Week 1: In Over My Head ***15***

Week 2: A Different Kind of Throne ***31***

Week 3: Grace for the Bedtime Hour ***45***

Week 4: Love You More ***59***

Week 5: Why Can't You Be More Helpful? ***73***

Week 6: To Fight or Not to Fight ***89***

Week 7: Are We There Yet? ***105***

Week 8: Can I? ***119***

Week 9: A Sigh of Relief ***133***

Week 10: I Don't Know How ***151***

Week 11: Ice Cream and A Good Cry ***165***

Week 12: Do You Hear Me? ***181***

Week 13: Oh, Crumb! ***197***

Week 14: So Many Choices ***211***

Week 15: Three Little Words ***227***

Week 16: Be Where Your Feet Are ***243***

YOUR INVITATION TO HOPE

To the mom with a messy bun wearing workout clothes (whether you actually intend to work out or not, it's not for me to know).
To the mom wearing a blazer and cute pumps.
To the mom with no make-up on.
To the mom with perfect make-up.
To the mom covered in tattoos.
To the mom whose minivan is filled with kids, shoes, toys, sports equipment, and old snacks.
To the mom who buys only organic.
To the mom on food stamps.
To the mom who nursed her baby.
To the mom who used formula.
To the stressed-out mom.
To the mom who thrives in motherhood.
To the adoptive mom, foster mom, single mom, biological mom, stepmom, working mom, home school mom, stay-at-home mom, or some combination of any of the above.

Whatever you look like, wherever you live, whatever kind of parenting style you use—this devotional is for you!

Chances are you second guess (maybe more often than you care to admit) whether you're doing this #MOMLIFE thing effectively. If you were able to sit down long enough to think, you'd most likely ponder ways to do things better than you currently are. You might read a few parenting blogs and set more goals. You might pin some helpful tips on Pinterest and tell yourself that this time you'll actually implement them. But the truth is we don't often have time to just sit and think. We are busy multitasking, raising kids, and trying not to drive ourselves crazy with worry.

This devotional is written with you (and your limited free time) in mind. In these pages you'll find a collection of truths from God's Word, lessons I'm learning as I'm (imperfectly) raising my own crew, and reflection prompts designed to allow God's Word to speak to your individual life and situation as well.

Each week we will look at one verse or passage of scripture for five days—learning from it, growing from its wisdom, and contemplating how we can apply the principles we find to our everyday lives. At the end of each of the five days, you'll find two longer passages between five and fifteen verses in length that you can read for further study before next week's devotional begins.

I pray that as you read ***#MOMLIFE*** for the next 16 weeks, you'll feel strengthened, encouraged, and more connected—first and foremost to the God who dearly loves you, then to yourself and the individuality and giftings that God has given you, and finally to other moms from all walks of life who are facing many of the same challenges right along with you.

We have differences that make us unique, but we also have similarities that join us together. This #MOMLIFE is hard work! We all want to do our best by our families. We all feel overwhelmed at times, overjoyed in others. Sometimes, I want to pull my hair out, scream, or do both, and I'm guessing I'm probably not alone in that! We hustle to get it all done. There are rarely dull moments, and whenever we might find one, some sort of radar goes off in our children's brains and they come running, asking, arguing, and needing—at least it seems that way!

So stop for a moment, grab some coffee, or maybe just a deep breath, and let's go on this journey of motherhood together. This #MOMLIFE is worth it, and you're not alone. Join us.

#MOMLIFE DEVOTIONAL

Overwhelmed

• WEEK ONE •

Week One

In Over My Head

> "Don't be afraid, I've redeemed you. I've called your name. You're mine. When you're in over your head, I'll be there with you. When you're in rough waters, you will not go down. When you're between a rock and a hard place, it won't be a dead end—Because I am God, your personal God, The Holy of Israel, your Savior. I paid a huge price for you: all of Egypt, with rich Cush and Seba thrown in! *That's* how much you mean to me! *That's* how much I love you! I'd sell off the whole world to get you back, trade the creation just for you."
>
> ***Isaiah 43:2-4 (TM)***

Despite my best intentions, I can often feel overwhelmed—especially in this season of life where my four kids still need so much. Between their sports schedules, school and homework, cooking and other housework, hobbies like exercise and writing, making time for friends and ministry—not to mention just getting my bed made—life often feels like it's just whizzing right by me. I try to be organized and make daily and weekly to-do lists on my phone to help myself out, but even then, it sometimes seems I still can't keep up.

One particular morning was especially a rough. My boys were grumpy, complaining, and nagging each other while the two oldest were getting ready for school. They couldn't find the socks they each wanted (because I hadn't done the laundry yet), they weren't happy with how their hair looked, and they were arguing over whose turn it was to take the dog out—and just about everything else.

They finally made it downstairs to the kitchen to pour their cereal while I dashed upstairs to dress my youngest son. I returned to find the boys sitting there with far-too-large piles of cereal in their bowls. They had been getting their own cereal for quite some time and knew the correct amount to pour, but this morning they decided to take advantage of the unexpected lack of supervision while I was briefly away.

I sighed and surveyed the situation. I wasn't too worried about my oldest son; he could woof down three bowls of cereal if I let him. But the two middle boys are light breakfast eaters. I know it and they know it, yet here they were each with huge bowls of cereal. Even worse, all three of them seemed to think it was funny, so I looked past their grins and right up into their eyes. "You better make sure to eat all of it, then!" My already elevated voice got louder as I went off on a rant about wasting food and money. I was *not* happy.

Sure enough, about halfway through their heaping bowls, the light-eating duo started complaining about how much their tummies hurt. Oh, the whining that ensued. Then, when I told my seven-year-old to finish his last few bites, he stood right up, marched over, put his unfinished bowl of cereal in the sink, and walked away.

My mouth literally dropped open. I was shocked at his act of defiance. It was quite unusual for him but seemed perfectly suited for the way the morning was going. *All I wanted to do was trust them with that one thing, to pour their cereal the right way while I was upstairs. And they couldn't even do that!* I was fuming—but more than that, I felt defeated. I shut the family devotion book I usually read to them at breakfast and told the boys to get in the car so that I could take the two oldest to school.

Questions swirled through my head as I drove. *What am I doing wrong? How can my kids act so disrespectfully? What makes them deliberately disobey a direct request? Am I an awful mom?* Still, I settled down enough to calmly remind my seven-year-old that there was going to be a consequence for his defiance, then hugged and kissed him as I dropped him off at school.

As my younger two sons and I walked back into our front door, my five-year-old ran upstairs, grabbed his dinosaur "piggy" bank, and asked me to open it. He then took out a handful of change and handed it to me. "It's to help pay for the cereal that we didn't eat," he said. I almost burst into tears. His pure heart that wanted to fix something he felt they had done wrong stopped me in my tracks.

Parenting is hard—most of the time! Sometimes it's the everyday stuff of being a mom that wears us down and makes us tired even before the day begins. Tantrums. Bad attitudes. Grumpy kids. Grumpy mom. Then I think of those moms who deal with the same stuff but have a special needs child, or are divorced or single, or are dealing with some sort of tragedy simultaneously. Motherhood is not easy. In all the moments where we feel ourselves coming undone, encouragement is crucial. So, when I came across this week's passage in Isaiah, I underlined it and took a moment to thank God for it. He's with us! When we wonder about our abilities, He's there to guide and comfort us, while providing wisdom, strength, grace, and help.

Let's Pray:

Father, so much about being a mom is overwhelming. Many times throughout my day I don't focus on the fact that You are always with me. I pray for a greater awareness of that fact. Thank You for the help that You graciously offer. Thank You that You haven't left me to figure this mom-life out on my own. Help me to turn to You when I'm in over my head. I am so grateful that You truly are a personal God. In Jesus' Name, Amen.

DAILY REFLECTION

Day 1

"When you pass through the waters, I will be with you. When you cross rivers, you will not drown. When you walk through fire, you will not be burned, nor will the flames hurt you. This is because I, the Lord, am your God, the Holy One of Israel, your Savior."

Isaiah 43:2-3a (NCV)

This week we'll look at other overwhelming situations and take time to let the truth of God's Word encourage our hearts.

1. Write about one recent circumstance that caused you to feel "in over your head" as a mom.

2. What is your typical response to feeling overwhelmed?

3. Why do you tend to react that way? For example, is it because you feel alone, incapable, unseen, hopeless, or out of control?

4. Looking again at Isaiah 43:2-3a above, underline the four things in verse 2 that God says will or will not happen when we face overwhelming circumstances.

5. In verse 3, God explains *why* He promises those to us. Below, write out that explanation.

DAILY REFLECTION

Day 2

"When you go through deep waters, I will be with you. When you go through rivers of difficulty, you will not drown. When you walk through the fire of oppression, you will not be burned up; the flames will not consume you. For I am the Lord, your God, the Holy One of Israel, your Savior."

Isaiah 43:2-3a (NLT)

1. This passage is inspiring in every translation, but today let's focus on the phrases *deep waters, rivers of difficulty,* and *the fire of oppression.* Write down something in your life that currently fits into one of these categories.

2. When was a time where you have seen the faithfulness of God at work in the midst of difficulty?

3. Take a moment and thank God for that.

4. Also, for the next few minutes, pray about the thing(s) you wrote about in answer to question 1. If you're not sure how to pray about it, pray the words of this passage. "God, as I am going through deep waters in the area of ________, I trust that You are with me. Thank You that You are my Savior."

5. As you wrap up this time of reflection today, write out Isaiah 43:2-3a. Place it somewhere you will see it this week and be reminded often of God's promises to you.

DAILY REFLECTION

Day 3

"When you go through deep waters and great trouble, I will be with you. When you go through rivers of difficulty, you will not drown! When you walk through the fire of oppression, you will not be burned up—the flames will not consume you. For I am the Lord your God, your Savior, the Holy One of Israel."
Isaiah 43:2-3a (TLB)

I began this week with a more lighthearted story about the stresses of motherhood and the chaos that can overwhelm our emotions. Today, I want to go a bit deeper.

Many of you might be facing all those struggles of motherhood *and* ________________. The thing about motherhood is that we don't really get a break from it to deal with the other things that invade our lives.

A few years ago, I sat in a doctor's office with my mom. Her cancer had returned and by the time it was diagnosed, it had progressed to Stage 4. When the doctor said she had four to six months left, I felt like I couldn't breathe.

We had been at the oncologist's office for quite a while, so shortly after I heard the news, I had to head to the car to pump my breast milk. The youngest of my four boys was just seven months old. I excused myself, went into the car, got situated, and *lost* it. I cried so hard it physically hurt. I wanted to scream and throw my pump across the parking lot, but there I sat—sobbing away, listening to the incessant drone of the pump.

My mom outlived that diagnosis by one month, and those seven months were the hardest of my life. She was declining right before my eyes and I could do nothing to stop it. I wanted to be at every appointment with her. She needed me many times for different things throughout the week, so of course, I went. I *wanted* to go—but I also felt the pull of the other demands in my life. My four young sons needed me. Things like school lunches still had to be done every day. My husband, as wonderful and understanding as he is, needed me to be present sometimes. I was the children's pastor and women's ministry director at our church. To say I was overwhelmed is an understatement. There just didn't seem to be enough time for it all. Time did what time does and kept marching on, so many days I felt stretched beyond what I could carry.

That's why I love this passage of Scripture. In the deepest waters I had ever walked in, God was with me every step of the way, offering His guidance, strength, comfort, and grace so that I could continue facing each day.

1. Is there anything in your life right now that is stretching you beyond what you feel capable of carrying?

2. Has God shown you anything this week as you've been reflecting on this passage of Scripture from Isaiah? If so, write it down below.

3. In all the translations of Isaiah 43:2-3a that we've looked at so far this week, I count the same nine guarantees in each one. I've listed the first three. Please finish the list in the space provided.

    1. We will go through deep waters and hard times.
    2. God will be with us.
    3. We will go through rivers of difficulty.
    4.
    5.
    6.
    7.
    8.
    9.

4. Do you find it comforting that God not only promises to be with us in the hard times, but also lets us know that we *will* go through those hard times. Explain your answer.

5. List the phrases and/or words of the verses that resonate with you the most. Meditate on these today.

DAILY REFLECTION

Day 4

"When you pass through the waters, I will be with you; And through the rivers, they will not overwhelm you. When you walk through fire, you will not be scorched, Nor will the flame burn you. For I am the Lord your God, The Holy One of Israel, your Savior."

Isaiah 43:2-3a (AMP)

1. What is one way you can apply this week's passage *practically* to your everyday life?

2. In these verses of Scripture, we find hope for the hard seasons and moments, but what I love even more is that our hope has a Name. It's not just an empty hope. It's not just wishful thinking. That name is found in verse three. Underline it in the passage of Scripture above.

3. The Lord our God and Savior is our hope. It's a hope we can build our lives on and around. It's a hope that sustains us when circumstances appear bleak, and it's a hope that lives in us as followers of Christ. Describe how a *living* hope can sustain you through the roughest of times.

4. Hebrews 13:5b says, "Never will I leave you; never will I forsake you." (NIV) This verse echoes the same promise found in this week's passage of Scripture. Below, share how this promise speaks to your heart.

5. Take a few moments to write yourself an encouraging note based off of Isaiah 43:2-3a.

DAILY REFLECTION

Day 5—Wrap Up

> "Don't be afraid, I've redeemed you. I've called your name. You're mine. When you're in over your head, I'll be there with you. When you're in rough waters, you will not go down. When you're between a rock and a hard place, it won't be a dead end—Because I am GOD, your personal God, The Holy of Israel, your Savior. I paid a huge price for you: all of Egypt, with rich Cush and Seba thrown in! *That's* how much you mean to me! *That's* how much I love you! I'd sell off the whole world to get you back, trade the creation just for you."
>
> ***Isaiah 43:2-4 (TM)***

Motherhood is challenging and definitely overwhelming at times. We are always mothers no matter how old our children get. When life is chaotic and hard, we have no choice but to handle the difficult things that come our way while still mothering our kids. Thankfully, in the midst of it all, we are not alone. God is continually working on our behalf—in us and for us. Take comfort in that. He has prepared us for the hard times by letting us know that they will come and by promising to be with us through them. As long as God is with us, we have all we need to face whatever comes our way.

As we wrap up our time of reflection this week, my prayer for you is that you will be reminded today that God has you in the palm of His hand. He is with you and He'll never leave you. Be encouraged in His presence.

Read God's Word

Over the next two days, I recommend you read Joshua 1:6-9 and Psalm 23.

#MOMLIFE DEVOTIONAL

Help!

• WEEK TWO •

Week Two

A Different Kind of Throne

"So then, since we have a great High Priest who has entered heaven, Jesus the Son of God, let us hold firmly to what we believe. This High Priest of ours understands our weaknesses, for he faced all of the same testings we do, yet he did not sin. So let us come boldly to the throne of our gracious God. There we will receive his mercy, and we will find grace to help us when we need it most."

Hebrews 4:14-16 (NLT)

It was a different kind of throne, and yet help was needed all the same.

My three-year-old charged past me toward the bathroom. Never mind that he had just told me again how he did *not* have to go. His beeline explained that he had held it as long as he possibly could.

I helped him get in there, then he quickly shooed me away. Several minutes later I went to the door. "Are you okay?" I called as my nose wrinkled to the all-too-familiar scent of the occasion. "Yep, mom. I'm fine!" he assured. I remained in the hall and a bit more time passed before I asked again, receiving the same response while noting that the odor seemed stronger than usual. I stood there and gave him a little longer before deciding to open the door.

I took one step into the bathroom and froze. My son was half naked and doing his best to clean up an explosion that hadn't quite made it into the toilet but *was* all over the commode and his clothing. In each hand he held a single square of toilet paper that he had gotten wet to help him with the task. *Two* little squares and one big, yucky mess! The determination on his face was evident—and it broke my heart. He knew I was standing outside the door the entire time, yet not once did he ask for my help.

He looked up at me cautiously with his big, brown eyes. "I got this Mama," he said, matter-of-factly. "You can go." I told him I could help and asked why he hadn't asked me to. "I not want you to be angry at me," he responded in his precious toddler lingo. "I can clean this up. You don't have to. I not want you to be mad."

Tears literally filled my eyes, and it had nothing to do with the smell. I have been known to huff and puff when my kids spill their milk at meals in their rambunctious carelessness, and I was certain that's what my son had in mind. But in that moment, I wasn't frustrated at all. Instead, I saw a sweet boy determined to clean up his own mess yet lacking the means to do so. He absolutely needed my help. He just didn't want to admit he did and was nervous about my reaction.

Even though it leaned me closer to the stinky disaster, I got down on one knee, looked him right in the eye, and assured him that I was *not* mad, and that I wanted to help him. I then gave him a big hug, got the cleaning and disinfecting supplies that we needed, and we went to work on the clean-up. Together.

How often have I approached God with the same view—feeling discouraged and overwhelmed by the predicaments *I* created yet trying to get rid of them on my own. Not wanting God to be disappointed with me, I pull away from His presence.

But the truth is, God loves us. He knows we are not perfect. Did you catch that? You are not expected to be perfect! God knows our weaknesses and shortcomings, and He is not disappointed or angry with us. Instead, He extends the offer of His divine intervention, willing to get right down into the filth, remove it with His grace, and cleanse it completely as though it never happened. No fumes, no fuss. He's just waiting for us to ask Him.

As our Heavenly Father, *He* is the perfect parent. I may get it right some of the time, but He gets it right all of the time. This week's passage tells us to approach His throne of *grace* (not anger, not justice, not eternal disappointment) so that we can receive the help that He longs to give. Trying to live our lives successfully without His help is as futile as my son trying to clean up his explosion with two squares of toilet paper.

We need God's help—so surrender the squares! He does not withdraw from messy situations or messy people. You can allow Him in or you can continue to stubbornly strive in your own limited efforts. The choice is yours.

Let's Pray:

Father, thank you that Your help is readily available to me. Many times, as I'm going about my day, I forget this truth. Today I say, "I need Your help!" Thank You that I don't have to have everything all together before I can come to You. Your lovingkindness allows me to come just as I am and receive the wisdom, patience, peace, joy, strength, grace, or understanding that I need in each of the situations I find myself in today. I'm looking to You, Lord. In Jesus' Name, Amen.

DAILY REFLECTION

Day 1

"Therefore, since we have a great high priest who has passed through the heavens—Jesus the Son of God—let us hold fast to our confession. For we do not have a high priest who is unable to sympathize with our weaknesses, but one who has been tempted in every way as we are, yet without sin. Therefore, let us approach the throne of grace with boldness, so that we may receive mercy and find grace to help us in time of need."

Hebrews 4:14-16 (CSB)

1. Is it hard for you to ask for and/or receive help? Explain your answer.

2. Do you enlist *God's* help in your daily mothering? If so, how and when? If not, why?

3. Do you believe as a mom that you're supposed to have it all figured out on your own? In light of your answer, how does this passage of Scripture illuminate God's truth into your thought process?

4. Think about a time where you stubbornly held onto your own way, all the while knowing you needed help. Write about it below.

5. What kept you from seeking God's help during that time?

DAILY REFLECTION

Day 2

"We have a great high priest, who has gone into heaven, and he is Jesus the Son of God. That is why we must hold on to what we have said about him. Jesus understands every weakness of ours, because he was tempted in every way that we are. But he did not sin! So whenever we are in need, we should come bravely before the throne of our merciful God. There we will be treated with undeserved kindness, and we will find help."

Hebrews 4:14-16 (CEV)

1. From reading our weekly passage again today, fill in the blanks: Jesus understands _________ _________ of ours, because he was tempted in every way that we are.

2. Do you ever worry that God doesn't understand/see/know/hear about the things you are facing? Explain your answer.

3. Our passage this week explains that *because* Christ faced every temptation we do, He *understands* our weaknesses and *desires* to help us. In the passage above, circle the two words that verse 16 says we will be treated with when we come before the throne of our merciful God.

4. Write about a time you know God helped you through.

5. Take some time right now to ask the Lord for His help. Whatever you have going on at this moment, take it to Him and seek His guidance. He is longing to help.

DAILY REFLECTION

Day 3

> "Since we have a great high priest, Jesus the Son of God, who has gone into heaven, let us hold on to the faith we have. For our high priest is able to understand our weaknesses. He was tempted in every way that we are, but he did not sin. Let us, then, feel very sure that we can come before God's throne where there is grace. There we can receive mercy and grace to help us when we need it."
>
> ***Hebrews 4:14-16 (NCV)***

1. Last week, we read Hebrews 13:5b-6 in the daily reflections. Let's look at these verses again today because on this journey of motherhood we are all on, this is a needed reminder.

Read Hebrews 13:5b-6:

> "For God has said, 'I will never fail you. I will never abandon you.' So we can say with confidence, 'The Lord is my helper, so I will have no fear. What can mere people do to me?'" (NLT)

Sometimes it seems like *my kids* are the "mere people," and in those moments, my answer is "a lot!" Okay, I'm kidding. Mostly.

I love the promise found in these verses. God will always be with us. Therefore, we have His help readily available at any moment. What a realization! Yet sometimes

I'm too busy cleaning up messes and trying to get my little brood in line and organized in my own easily exhaustible strength that I forget to ask for that help, *His* help. But oh, how I need it.

Today, I hope these verses encourage you as much as they encourage me. We do not have to do this mom-life in our own strength. That is such a refreshing truth.

2. What fears do you have as a mom that Hebrews 13:5b-6 speaks to?

3. On a scale from 1-10 (1 being the least and 10 being the greatest), how likely are you to go through your day aware that God is with you and that He will never fail you?

4. How does this knowledge affect the way you mother your kids?

5. What are some things that you could remember today that would get that number on the scale a little higher?

DAILY REFLECTION

Day 4

"Therefore, since we have a great high priest who has ascended into heaven, Jesus the Son of God, let us hold firmly to the faith we profess. For we do not have a high priest who is unable to empathize with our weaknesses, but we have one who has been tempted in every way, just as we are—yet he did not sin. Let us then approach God's throne of grace with confidence, so that we may receive mercy and find grace to help us in our time of need."

Hebrews 4:14-16 (NIV)

1. Fill in the blanks: Verse 16 tells us we can approach God's throne of _________ with _________ so that we may receive mercy and find grace to _________ us in our time of need.

2. How does it encourage you to know that God invites you to approach Him with confidence?

3. Make a list of specific things where you could currently use God's help.

4. Spend some time in prayer today about this list.

5. Make a note or set an alarm to remind yourself to pray *throughout* your day for God's guidance. This could be done with Post-it Notes or index cards placed strategically where you'll come across them during your day. I often get brightly-colored index cards, write verses and reminders on them, and put them up in my bedroom, bathroom, and closet. One of the notes I've left for myself simply says, "Hey, pray!" I never do too many at once because then it will feel like clutter, but I love to keep a few up. I encourage you to try it out.

DAILY REFLECTION

Day 5—Wrap-Up

"So then, since we have a great High Priest who has entered heaven, Jesus the Son of God, let us hold firmly to what we believe. This High Priest of ours understands our weaknesses, for he faced all of the same testings we do, yet he did not sin. So let us come boldly to the throne of our gracious God. There we will receive his mercy, and we will find grace to help us when we need it most."

Hebrews 4:14-16 (NLT)

Like my son, we often slip into "I'll just do it myself" mode. For whatever reason (fear of disappointment, busyness, pride, stubbornness, etc.), we don't take the time to seek God's help and we exhaust ourselves in the process. We may be able to get by for a while like this, but eventually we will wear out.

When it comes to us as moms needing to help our kids, we get it. When it comes to us as moms needing to help ourselves, we don't. Let's not get stuck obstinately holding onto our two squares. We were not created to be perfect, so let's make the choice today to boldly approach His throne *together*, finding the grace and help that we need so we can be the best moms we can be.

Read God's Word

Over the next two days, I recommend you read Psalm 18:30-36 and Matthew 7:7-11.

#MOMLIFE DEVOTIONAL

Grace

• **WEEK** THREE •

Week three

Grace for the Bedtime Hour

"'My grace is all you need. My power works best in weakness.' So now I am glad to boast about my weaknesses, so that the power of Christ can work through me."

2 Corinthians 12:9b (NLT)

From his bed, my oldest son started yelling first.

"I want a hug and kiss, mom!"

I had already given my boys several hugs and kisses before I had left their room. They were all *finally* in bed with the lights off, their blankets on, and all I wanted to do was wait long enough to know they were settled and then slip downstairs.

Honestly, bedtime can get the best of me sometimes. Somewhere in that span of time between their dinner dishes going into the sink and their eyelids finally closing with sleep, craziness tends to happen! For years, we've had the same bedtime routine most nights: bath or shower, pajamas, floss and brush teeth, and get in bed. Yet nearly every night it still seems that I find myself repeating these reminders while they wildly dance around naked like they have no idea what they're supposed to be doing. They just look at me with confusion in their eyes each time I ask them again why they don't have their pajamas on yet. No wonder I rarely think about things like cleaning out their ears or clipping their nails.

I've never actually had to herd cattle or sheep, but I imagine it must feel a lot like trying to get four boys into bed.

On this particular night, it was my oldest son who found a reason to try to bring me back into his room. "Hug and kiss, mama," he kept calling, obviously trying to stall. I should cherish every single second they want to hug and kiss me, but all I desperately craved was simply some time to myself. So, instead of sweetly going in to hug and kiss the boys yet again, I went into my bedroom, which was just around the corner from their rooms, and ducked into the closet.

I know...real mature, right? I'd never done it before. But there I was, a grown woman playing hide-and-seek in hopes they'd give up calling for me and go to sleep so I could enjoy some peace and quiet.

But it wasn't to be. All four started the same "hug and kiss" mantra. Then, I heard one of my middle sons get out of bed and venture into the hallway. I turned the closet light off but kept the door cracked just enough, hoping he'd think I went downstairs. Then I saw his little mouth press right up to the crack. "Mom? We want another hug and kiss. Are you in there? Why are you ignoring us?"

I actually started laughing at the ridiculousness I'd just tried, eased open the door, and followed him back to their bedrooms. I *did* hug and kiss them, but it was begrudgingly at best—and they knew it. "Okay (hug and kiss) now goodnight (hug and kiss) go to sleep (hug and kiss)." My oldest exasperatedly said, "Geez," expressing the sentiment shared by all four of them at the way I was storming around.

Whether or not you have one child or ten, little or big, motherhood is definitely a challenge. There are so many ways we can fall short in our selfishness and limited ability. I am grateful to be a mom, and I love my kids more than life itself.

However, there are days where I just come *undone* at the tasks before me.

In those moments where I don't act like the mom I want to be, I have found it so easy to pile guilt onto my already full plate. I'm fairly certain other moms are pretty good at this, too. But that's not what God wants us to do. Instead of diving into our guilt, He wants us to dive into His grace!

As I helped my sleepy-eyed boys get dressed the next morning, I got down to their eye level and apologized for being so upset the night before. Then I gave them the kind of hugs and kisses I should've in the first place, and the smiles they gave me in return were priceless.

I won't always get it right, and neither will you. We will make mistakes, rush when we should slow down, react in frustration, and disappoint our kids. Yet the way we handle our mistakes also teaches our sons and daughters how they can handle theirs. I am so thankful for God's grace in the midst of my weaknesses, for lessons learned, and for the privilege of being a mom, even with all its challenges.

Let's Pray:

Father, I know I don't always get it right when it comes to mothering the kids You've given me. I fall short, I lose my cool, I run out of patience, I react in selfishness, and then I regret it. I ask that You continue to teach me how to lean into You more throughout my day. You have offered me Your help, strength, and wisdom, and I desperately need it. I pray that You would enable me to be the kind of mother that honors You with my words and actions. I know that comes from spending time with You, so here I am, Father, coming to You, ready to receive. In Jesus' Name, Amen.

DAILY REFLECTION

Day 1

"'My grace is sufficient for you, for power is perfected in weakness.' Most gladly, therefore, I will rather boast about my weaknesses, so that the power of Christ may dwell in me."

2 Corinthians 12:9b (NASB)

1. Describe in a few sentences what the bedtime routine looks like at your house.

2. Is there a time of day where your patience wanes or your stress level tends to rise the most? Write about it below.

3. Why does that time of day seem more difficult than others?

4. What are your typical responses during those moments?

5. How does our verse for the week encourage you today?

DAILY REFLECTION

Day 2

"'My kindness is all you need. My power is strongest when you are weak.' So if Christ keeps giving me his power, I will gladly brag about how weak I am."

2 Corinthians 12:9b (CEV)

1. In what areas do you feel weakest as a mom?

2. List some ways that you have seen God come through for you despite these weaknesses.

3. According to 2 Corinthians 12:9, when is God's power most evident in our lives?

4. Do you have a hard time believing and receiving that truth? If so, explain why below?

5. Using our weekly verse, take a moment to write a statement of encouragement that you could share with another mom friend. (Ask God to give you the opportunity to share it.)

DAILY REFLECTION

Day 3

> "'My grace is enough to cover and sustain you. My power is made perfect in weakness.' So ask me about my thorn, inquire about my weaknesses, and I will gladly go on and on—I would rather stake my claim in these and have the power of the Anointed One at home within me."
>
> ***2 Corinthians 12:9b (THE VOICE)***

Conversely to the story I shared in this week's devotional, there are many other nights that I stand in the doorways of my kids' rooms and watch them sleep with tears in my eyes. They look so peaceful and sweet, and as I look at them I'm reminded of the priceless gift they are to me.

Why is it I often forget that while they're awake? When there's arguing, competing, wrestling, dirty laundry, and homework that needs to be done and dinner that needs to be cooked, I tend to react, and overreact, in frustration. Countless times I have made a resolution not to yell. I don't want to be a mom who yells. I've written it down, set goals, and come up with better ways to express myself, but in the heat of the moment it all goes out the window and I say things in a tone I'm not proud of.

I desire to be a great mom and to raise kids who love the Lord and who know they are loved in return. But I often wonder if the desires in my heart are actually connecting to the (often chaotic) reality around me.

The truth is that God does not intend for us to do motherhood alone. His plan has always been that we would live life leaning into His strength. When you feel the weakness of your own humanity, don't despair! Our verse this week continues to serve as our reminder that God's limitless resources are always available to us. His grace can and will sustain us through whatever we face whenever we face it.

1. Using the translation of 2 Corinthians 12:9 that we read today, fill in the blanks: My grace is enough to_________ and _________ you.

2. How does the statement, "God's grace is enough," affect you? How does it make you feel? How does it challenge you? Write out your answers.

3. What is one way you can be intentional about allowing God's grace to cover and sustain you today?

4. Write about an instance in which God's grace showed up in your life yesterday. You may not even have noticed at the time but take a moment to really think back on it now.

5. In light of that, offer a prayer of thanks.

DAILY REFLECTION

Day 4

"'My grace is sufficient for you, for my power is made perfect in weakness.' Therefore I will boast all the more gladly about my weaknesses, so that Christ's power may rest on me."
2 Corinthians 12:9b (NIV)

1. Your kids don't need a perfect mom. They need a mom who knows where to go (and where to teach *them* to go) to find the grace that sustains and strengthens. We do this by *leaving room* for God's power to show up in our weaknesses as we seek Him. You don't have to know all the answers. You have access to the One who does! If we don't take the time to intentionally draw close to God, we don't have the room for Him to work in our lives. How can you create space in your heart today for God's grace to carry you through?

2. Read Psalm 28:7:

   "The Lord is my strength and my [impenetrable] shield; My heart trusts [with unwavering confidence] in Him, and I am helped; Therefore my heart greatly rejoices, And with my song I shall thank Him and praise Him." (AMP)

3. Underline the parts of this verse that jump out to you the most. Explain how those words speak to your heart.

4. God's Word continues to confirm that He makes the way for us to be strengthened in the midst of our weakness. Name a current situation in which you need God's strength.

5. Take a moment and write out a prayer asking God for His grace and power to be magnified through your life today.

DAILY REFLECTION

Day 5—Wrap-Up

> "'My grace is all you need. My power works best in weakness.' So now I am glad to boast about my weaknesses, so that the power of Christ can work through me."
>
> ***2 Corinthians 12:9b (NLT)***

God makes provision for our weakness. Does that truth reassure you? I definitely find it comforting. His Word tells us that He equips us with His strength. We don't have to get stuck in our shortcomings.

We are all a mess sometimes! We have issues and situations we go through and deal with. We balance and juggle so much. Sometimes it's hard to live as though God's grace is enough, though it is.

Our weaknesses will either lead us to frustration and despair or to the One who knows how to guide us through them. When you find yourself in circumstances you don't know how to handle, allow God's grace to work. Draw close to Him during those times. Ask for His strength. Our weakness doesn't negate God's power. In fact, it magnifies it!

If you're feeling weak today, take a deep breath and be refreshed in the fact that you are in the perfect position to have God's grace activated in your life. Let's remind ourselves, and teach our kids in the process, that though we aren't perfect, the grace of God is our sustaining power.

Read God's Word

Over the next two days, I recommend you read Isaiah 40:26-31 and Ephesians 3:16-21.

#MOMLIFE DEVOTIONAL

Living Loved

• **WEEK** FOUR •

Week Four

Love You More

"See what great love the Father has lavished on us, that we should be called children of God! And that is what we are!"

1 John 3:1a (NIV)

One day in Target I had the privilege of overhearing a sweet conversation between a little girl and her mom. The daughter told her mother she loved her, the mom said it back, and then the little girl said, "I love you more."

The mother laughed. "That's not possible. I love *you* more."

On they went with their precious declarations of love until they walked down the next aisle and were out of earshot.

That little exchange between mom and child made me smile *and* want to burst into tears at the same time. That's a female for you, right? I delighted at their loving hearts and thought of the many times my boys and I said have said the same thing back and forth to each other. I always enjoy when they try to "out love" me. Over the years, we've come up with things like, "I love you as deep as the ocean," "as high as the sky," "as wide as the world," or "as tall as the tallest building."

But it also made me miss hearing those words from my own mom. She always ended every text conversation or phone call with, "Love you more." A few days before she passed away, she could barely speak, but I knew she had things she desperately wanted to tell me. I simply took her hand, kissed her, and told her

I loved her. She looked at me, and although the sound of the words couldn't be heard, slowly mouthed, "Love you more." That memory will forever be etched into my mind and heart.

As moms, I feel that we'll always love our kids more. No matter if they are in trouble, no matter if we are stressed, no matter if there is tension between us—those little, crazy, messy humans are a part of us. Even when they start walking around in teenage and adult bodies, they remain in our hearts so that we don't hesitate to tell them, "Love you more." I wholeheartedly believe that I love my kids more than they love me, and always will.

However, as a daughter, I like the feeling of *being* loved more. There is security in the fact that, no matter how old I am, I will be loved despite what I may do or get myself into. Now that I no longer have a living parent, I am thankful that I have a relationship with a God who feels the same way about me!

Sometimes we must remind ourselves that no matter how old we are, and no matter how many children or grandchildren we have, we are still daughters! According to Romans 8:14-17, if we've chosen to follow Christ, we've been adopted into His family. We are loved by a perfect Heavenly Father—and we were never meant to outgrow that role. We were designed by our Creator to live our lives knowing we are loved!

The Lord loves each of us far more than we could ever love Him. Maybe that's not the God you envision in your mind, or perhaps that's not the message you grew up hearing in church. But the Bible is filled with one example after another of a God who constantly declares to His people, "I love you more! I love you so much that I set up a plan to rescue you from the hopelessness around you and even from the messes you've put yourself into."

In the same way I want my kids to know to their core that they are loved, God wants you to know in your innermost being that He loves you more.

Let's Pray:

Father, thank You for loving me. You love me so much more than I even realize. Too often, I fail to recognize how Your love impacts my daily life. Today, I pray for a deeper understanding. I want to go through my days *living loved* so that I can also give love. Please help me to remember that no matter what other roles I have in life, I will always be a daughter in need of her perfect Heavenly Father. In Jesus' Name, Amen.

DAILY REFLECTION

Day 1

"See how very much our Father loves us, for he calls us his children, and that is what we are!"

1 John 3:1a (NLT)

1. Describe the view that you had growing up of God's love.

2. How has that view affected the way you approach God?

3. Do you find God's love for you hard or easy to accept? Explain your answer.

4. On a scale of 1-10 (1 being "very little" and 10 being "a whole lot"), how often do you live each day feeling confident *because* you know you are truly loved by God?

5. List a few hindrances that have held you back from confidently *living loved.*

DAILY REFLECTION

Day 2

"See what an incredible quality of love the Father has shown to us, that we would [be permitted to] be named and called and counted the children of God! And so we are!"

1 John 3:1a (AMP)

1. Do you identify with being called a "child of God?" Describe the feelings that stir within you reading that title?

2. Has your own childhood had a part to play in your ability to walk in the identity God has given you, even as an adult?

3. What is one thing you can do right now to help you live more fully present in your role as a *daughter* in need of her Heavenly Father's love?

4. Below, rewrite our verse for the week in first person. For example, you could start by writing, "See what an incredible quality of love the father has shown to **me** that **I** would..." Then read it out loud to yourself like you believe it!

5. Take a moment to pray and ask God to help you *live loved* today.

DAILY REFLECTION

Day 3

"Think how much the Father loves us. He loves us so much that he lets us be called his children, as we truly are."

1 John 3:1a (CEV)

I struggle to live like I'm loved daily. It's more comfortable to live within the confines of what I think I can control, but God draws me into something deeper. Something I can't control. A life of faith filled with extravagant love. We don't have to earn it. We can't lose it. We simply have to teach ourselves to live in it, and while that sounds easy, it's difficult to do. Our human nature fights against it. We feel unworthy. Distractions tug our hearts away. Doubts fill our minds.

Yet God continues inviting us to step beyond our comfort zones, trusting fully that He is who He says He is, that He does what He says He'll do, and that we are who He says we are. His daughters. Dearly loved. Chosen. Seen. Wanted. Cherished.

1. Read 1 John 4:9-11 below and underline each time the word *love* or *loved* are used.

    "God showed how much he loved us by sending his one and only Son into the world so that we might have eternal life through him. This is real love—not that we loved God, but that he loved us and sent his Son as a sacrifice to take away our sins. Dear friends, since God loved us that much, we surely ought to love each other." (NLT)

2. According to these Scriptures, how did God show His love for us?

3. What is our response to His love meant to be according to verse 11?

4. Do you find it difficult to love others? Explain your answer.

5. Spend a moment thanking God for His incredible love for you. While you are praying, ask God to give you an opportunity to show love to someone else today.

DAILY REFLECTION

Day 4

"Consider the kind of extravagant love the Father has lavished on us—He calls us children of God! It's true; we are His beloved children."

1 John 3:1a (THE VOICE)

1. Describe a time where you needed to remind yourself to *live loved*. Did you choose to do it? Explain the outcome either way.

2. Read Ephesians 3:16-19:

   "I pray that from his glorious, unlimited resources he will empower you with inner strength through his Spirit. Then Christ will make his home in your hearts as you trust in him. Your roots will grow down into God's love and keep you strong. And may you have the power to understand, as all God's people should, how wide, how long, how high, and how deep his love is. May you experience the love of Christ, though it is too great to understand fully. Then you will be made complete with all the fullness of life and power that comes from God." (NLT)

3. Fill in the blanks from verse 19 above. “May you ____________ the love of Christ, though it is too great to understand fully. _____ you will be made __________ with all the fullness of life and power that comes from God.”

4. We don’t have to fully understand God’s love in order to a) experience it, and b) be affected by it. His love is freely given to us and as we accept it, we become more whole, more complete. How does this truth encourage you?

5. Go through Ephesians 3:16-19 again, and instead of just reading it, pray it over your own life. You could say, “Father, I ask that from Your glorious, unlimited resources You will empower me with inner strength through Your Spirit...” You may want to begin to pray these verses over yourself daily to help you live in the fullness of God’s love for you.

DAILY REFLECTION

Day 5—Wrap-Up

"See what great love the Father has lavished on us, that we should be called children of God! And that is what we are!"
1 John 3:1a (NIV)

God's love for us is extravagant. Romans 8:38 says, "And I am convinced that nothing can ever separate us from God's love." (NLT) Have you ever noticed that the word *nothing* is actually made up of the words *no thing*? There is no thing that can take away, hinder, or lessen God's love for you.

Even when you're feeling unseen, unappreciated, exhausted, and disappointed, God sees you and He loves you. Even when you're at your worst, God loves you. Even when you've isolated yourself from those around you, God loves you. NOTHING can separate you from His love!

We are His daughters, and because of that, He lavishes His love on us. Every day we can choose to live our lives loved by the Creator of the universe, allowing that love to overflow to all whom we come into contact! That is a wonderful truth.

You are loved. He loves you more. Believe it. Enjoy it. Live in it.

Read God's Word

Over the next two days, I recommend you read Romans 8:14-19, 31-39 and 1 John 4:7-19.

#MOMLIFE DEVOTIONAL

Perspective

• **WEEK** FIVE •

Week Five

Why Can't You Be More Helpful?

> "O Jacob, how can you say the Lord does not see your troubles? O Israel, how can you say God ignores your rights? Have you never heard? Have you never understood? The Lord is the everlasting God, the Creator of all the earth. He never grows weak or weary. No one can measure the depths of his understanding. He gives power to the weak and strength to the powerless."
>
> ***Isaiah 40:27-29 (NLT)***

To say the least, getting kids ready and out of the house in the morning can be a challenge. They need to eat, get dressed, brush their teeth, and comb and style their hair (and for me that's still true, even with boys)—not to mention fix lunches, fill water bottles, grab backpacks, and gather sports clothes for practice after school. Of all these things, the seemingly simplest one, finding socks, always seems to be a particularly excruciating ordeal.

Of course, none of this ever goes as smoothly as it should, or on the timetable I have available to me. Add a baby or toddler to the chaos, and mornings can quickly become hectic bordering on out of control.

On one such morning, the boys and I were rushing around trying to get everything done and I couldn't find a single pair of soccer socks that matched. Two of the boys had practice that afternoon, so there wasn't going to be a spare moment to come home and find the rogue socks between the end of school and start of practice. To top it all off, I was also missing one of the shin guards—and time was quickly slipping through my fingers like a David Beckham bender through a goalkeeper's hands.

I tore through my house like a whirlwind, checking the multiple dirty piles of clothes as well as the clean piles that had yet to be folded and put away. Between running around like crazy and repeatedly telling two of my boys to get their shoes on, I was beyond frustrated—way beyond!

I finally found the socks, located the missing shin guard, got the baby in his car seat carrier, grabbed my diaper bag, pump bag, and purse, and even took out the dogs—only to turn around to find one of my sons, *still* in his socks, playing with his Legos.

I felt like a volcano ready to blow, but I kept my cool as we made it into the car. Before I started pulling out of the driveway, I glanced in the rearview mirror and asked the same Lego-playing son if he had remembered to get his soccer ball. His wide eyes told me all I needed to know. Resisting the urge to let the smoke and lava spew, I calmly asked him to jump out and find the ball.

He sighed, glared at me, and said with an obviously frustrated voice, "Why can't you be more helpful, mom?"

I was speechless and, just like you've seen in a Looney Tunes cartoon, my mouth literally fell open. I could imagine the steam puffing from my ears, too. "*Excuse me?*" is all I could muster. I then stomped behind him inside the house (because, of course, I didn't want the neighbors to hear me) and proceeded to list, in exquisite detail, all the things I had just done *that very morning* to help him and his brothers.

Yes, I reacted. The words I said weren't hurtful, but my tone was. We drove in silence for about ten minutes until a little voice from the back seat apologized.

I was challenged that morning, in the aftermath of my own exasperation, to stop and reflect on all God had been doing in and through my own life. It was clear to me that day that because my son was preoccupied with his Legos, he missed all the things I was doing around the house on his behalf. How many times, due to my own daily distractions, have I neglected to realize God's faithfulness in my situations? How often have I vented in frustration when I can't sense His help? I know that has happened more times than I'd like to admit. Thankfully, God doesn't react in anger to us.

We can't always see God at work and can easily start questioning, "Where are you, Lord?" "Are you listening?" "How long?" "If you really love me, then why?" "Why can't you be more helpful?" But we can choose to trust that He *is* helping us. Regardless of how our circumstances look and how we feel, His Word tells us that He is aware, He understands, and He is continually strengthening and empowering us.

I'd like to extend to you the same challenge I was faced with that morning. The next time you find yourself ready to question God, stop and think of all the things He has done for you, and begin to thank Him. Spend time intentionally acknowledging His involvement in your life and watch how your perspective (and your attitude) start to shift.

Let's Pray:

God, you know that my heart is bent toward wanting my own way when I want it. I can tend to question and complain when I don't see the answers coming. Help me to remember that You are the mighty Creator of Heaven and Earth and You never grow tired. When I can't see the outcome yet, I'll praise anyway. When

I feel unsure, I'll trust in You. You understand all that I go through and You strengthen me for the journey. Thank You for Your ceaseless patience with me, Lord. In Jesus' Name, Amen.

DAILY REFLECTION

Day 1

"Family of Jacob, why do you complain, 'The Lord doesn't notice our condition'? People of Israel, why do you say, 'Our God doesn't pay any attention to our rightful claims'? Don't you know who made everything? Haven't you heard about him? The Lord is the God who lives forever. He created everything on earth. He won't become worn out or get tired. No one will ever know how great his understanding is. He gives strength to those who are tired. He gives power to those who are weak."

Isaiah 40:27-29 (NIRV)

1. Read the weekly passage: In the above passage, underline what Isaiah says that the Israelites (the family of Jacob) were complaining about.

2. How does it make you feel when your children start complaining about something you said or some decision you made?

3. Do you often find *yourself* venting complaints or frustrations to God? Explain your answer.

4. Take a moment to think about what God has done for you lately. Write out several examples. (If you can't think of specific things right away, think broader at first to get your mind going. Examples include: another day of life, provision for your needs, your family, your job, etc.)

5. Today, ask God to make you aware of His hand at work in your daily life.

DAILY REFLECTION

Day 2

"You people of Israel, say, 'God pays no attention to us! He doesn't care if we are treated unjustly.' But how can you say that? Don't you know? Haven't you heard? The Lord is the eternal God, Creator of the earth. He never gets weary or tired; his wisdom cannot be measured. The Lord gives strength to those who are weary."

Isaiah 40:27-29 (CEV)

1. What does a typical morning routine look like for you? Write it out.

2. Circle the option below that best finishes the following sentence truthfully for you.

As a mom I feel frazzled:

- Often
- Somewhat often
- Rarely

Use the space provided to explain the why behind your answer.

3. According to verse 28, how often does God get tired?

4. According to verse 29, what does God give those who are weary?

Chances are, you are doing a lot! They might seem like trivial things: buttering toast, wiping counters, finding lost items, carpooling, and giving kisses and hugs—but don't forget they represent a very significant thing, your love. Your love for these children is what causes you to take care of them, meet their needs, sacrifice sleep, wipe tears, listen when they need to talk, and laugh at their jokes even when they're not funny. Your love is vital! Be encouraged today by our passage of scripture. God will equip you with the things you need to be the mom He has called you to be.

5. Take a moment to write a reminder encouraging yourself that a) what you are doing matters in bigger ways than you can possibly see right now, and b) God will continue to strengthen you.

Feel free to reread that reminder as often as you need to!

DAILY REFLECTION

Day 3

> "Why would you ever complain, O Jacob, or, whine, Israel, saying, 'God has lost track of me. He doesn't care what happens to me'? Don't you know anything? Haven't you been listening? God doesn't come and go. God lasts. He's Creator of all you can see or imagine. He doesn't get tired out, doesn't pause to catch his breath. And he knows everything, inside and out. He energizes those who get tired, gives fresh strength to dropouts."
>
> ***Isaiah 40:27-29 (TM)***

1. Have you ever felt like God lost track of you? Explain your answer.

Isaiah was basically saying to the people of Israel, "Don't you understand who God is and all He's done for you? Don't overlook His goodness. He hasn't lost track of you. He's working on your behalf." But, like my son did with me, and like the Israelites did with God, we often pass over and miss the things He has done for us as well. When we can't see Him working things out we often feel like He isn't. Questioning God and asking Him questions are two different things. God invites us to come to Him.

Hebrews 4:16 says:

> "So let us come boldly to the throne of our gracious God. There we will receive his mercy, and we will find grace to help us when we need it most." (NLT)

Our faith is made stronger as we ask questions and seek the truth found in God's Word for answers. However, when we question God as though He owes us an explanation, our pride hardens our heart. The result of this is not a deeper faith but rather a critical spirit.

2. Can you think of a time when you approached God in one or both of these ways? Write about it below.

3. What was the outcome?

On Day 2, I mentioned several of the seemingly insignificant things we know we are doing for our families. Right now, let's direct our focus to many of the little things God does *for us* every day. Sometimes it takes a moment to reflect on that. His grace in our daily lives can seem mundane if we aren't intentional in recognizing it.

4. Think back on your day yesterday and write down how God was gracious to you.

5. From today's translation of our weekly passage, how does it make you feel to read, "God doesn't come and go. God lasts?"

We read from God's Word that He is continually with us. Before you close this devotional, offer a prayer of thanks for all He's doing in and through you right now, even if you can't see it.

DAILY REFLECTION

Day 4

> "Why do you say, O Jacob, And speak, O Israel: 'My way is hidden from the Lord, And my just claim is passed over by my God'? Have you not known? Have you not heard? The everlasting God, the Lord, The Creator of the ends of the earth, Neither faints nor is weary. His understanding is unsearchable. He gives power to the weak, And to those who have no might He increases strength."
>
> ***Isaiah 40:27-29 (NKJV)***

1. Read the last two verses of Isaiah 40 below and circle the group of people who experienced the blessing listed in these verses.

> "Even youths will become weak and tired, and young men will fall in exhaustion. But those who trust in the Lord will find new strength. They will soar high on wings like eagles. They will run and not grow weary. They will walk and not faint."
>
> ***Isaiah 40:30-31 (NLT)***

2. Do you consider yourself someone who trusts in the Lord?

3. If your answer was yes, then read through verses 30-31 again, replacing "they" with "I."

4. How does that encourage your heart today?

5. Let's help our hearts remain in a reflective state of gratitude. In the space provided, write a prayer of thanks to God for all the ways He blesses you. Pause and consider His provision for you this past week.

DAILY REFLECTION

Day 5—Wrap-Up

"O Jacob, how can you say the LORD does not see your troubles? O Israel, how can you say God ignores your rights? Have you never heard? Have you never understood? The Lord is the everlasting God, the Creator of all the earth. He never grows weak or weary. No one can measure the depths of his understanding. He gives power to the weak and strength to the powerless."

Isaiah 40:27-29 (NLT)

The everyday paths of life can seem mundane, but without them chaos would be the norm or even more normal than it already is. This *#MOMLIFE* we are living is the daily opportunity to show our love in hundreds of different ways. What you are doing matters even if no one else says it, so today, allow me. You're doing a great job, mama! Keep it up.

When discouragement and discontentment come knocking, and they do for us all, remind yourself that your God never tires of loving you and helping you. He sees you. He knows how to give you the strength you need when you're feeling weak. He is daily pouring His grace upon you. But just like our kids don't always notice all we do for them, we often miss all that God is doing for us. Let's make it a point to intentionally stop and reflect on it, not taking His presence in our everyday life for granted. I encourage you to make some space in this devotional or a separate journal to create a list where you can write as often as you can the ways you encounter God's grace at work in your daily life.

Read God's Word

Over the next two days, I recommend you read Romans 8:22-28 and 2 Corinthians 4:7-9, 13-18

#MOMLIFE DEVOTIONAL

Surrender

• WEEK SIX •

Week Six

To Fight or Not to Fight

"Come close to God, and God will come close to you."

James 4:8a (NLT)

The night light was on, its soft light casting a warm glow over the beach décor of my youngest son's room. With him in my arms, I sat down in the corner rocking chair, wishing I could transport myself to an Adirondack chair on that beach and be taken away by the sound of the waves. I looked at my son's face and let out an exhausted breath. His older brothers were already in bed—and I knew he was tired, too, but he was fighting it with all the strength his little ten-month-old body could muster.

I had done everything I usually did. I bathed him, let him sit in on story time with his brothers, fed him, and was now attempting to rock him in the quiet coziness of his room, but he wasn't having it. He just kept pushing, squirming, squealing, and kicking for about five minutes until the only thing left to do was give him his blanket and pacifier and lay him in his crib.

I knew he was going to cry. I knew he didn't want me to put him in the crib, but until he was ready to let me hold him it was all I *could* do. I stepped outside of his door and waited.

I wasn't far away. He wasn't alone, and just seconds earlier he was trying to push himself away from me with all his might. But his cry signaled that he wanted me. The same arms which seemed confining to him moments ago were now highly desired compared to the relative freedom of his crib.

So I walked back in and picked up my frustrated, exhausted little son—and this time, he did not fight me. He snuggled into the side of my neck and allowed me to sit with him and calm him down. Within minutes he was fast asleep on my chest. I closed my eyes and held him, breathing in the soothing scent of his lavender baby lotion, and recalled how overwhelmed I had felt when I first found out I was pregnant with this fourth child. *I already had three wild and rowdy boys. How was I going to handle another one? Could I still be a good mom for four kids?* Yet God knew better than I did. Through Him, I have been a good mom and handled my crazy quartet. I rocked with him nuzzled against me thankful anew to be a child of God.

We fight God ourselves sometimes. We put up our defenses, build our walls, and have our attitudes. We think we don't need the Lord. We convince ourselves that His ways are confining, His demands are too high, and His approval unattainable. We believe we can do better living life on our own terms—but God is a perfect and patient Father. He is never far away.

Are you feeling lonely? Frustrated? Like the weight of your world is on your shoulders? Stop fighting and surrender. Come close. Lean in. Whether you've been struggling with the mere existence of God, the reality of His love, or the nearness of His presence in your everyday life, stop striving.

Allow the hands that formed you and shaped the world to now lead you to a quiet place of truth and refreshment. As you do, you will experience a peace that goes beyond reason, heals the heart, and soothes the soul. It sparks hope into the darkest of circumstances. That peace equips you to hold on and keep going.

We know that we cannot be strong *all* the time or in *every* circumstance. Could it be that there is a Strength that doesn't grow weary? Could it be that we've been resisting the very Life that we actually want? Have we built up walls against the very Answer to our problems?

As I sat holding my son that night, I was reminded again to surrender. In most aspects of life, surrender is equated with losing, but this is not so when it comes to Jesus. With Him, surrender equals life, freedom, peace, purpose, hope, and so much more.

Don't just take my word for it. The only thing my son needed to do was reach up his arms to me, and I was going to do the rest. Right now, lift your heart up to the One who is longing to draw you close—and He will. Whether it's your first time, or the first time in a long time, He will *always* come close to you when you reach out to Him.

Let's Pray:

God, help me to see You as the perfect, loving Father that You are. It requires faith and trust to let go and surrender to You. Help me to do this daily. It's my nature to want to control, and I find myself pulling away from You when I'm busy, stressed, and exhausted. I've seen my children do this so many times with me, but I often know what they need even if they can't see it or want to admit it. Help me to remember that You have the same loving knowledge and care about me. I choose to lean in closer to you today, God, and trust that as I do You're going to take me up into Your loving arms. In Jesus' Name, Amen.

DAILY REFLECTION

Day 1

"Come near to God, and he will come near to you."

James 4:8a (CEV)

1. Think about a time when your own child pulled away from you. What caused him or her to withdraw? How did it make you feel as a mom?

2. If your child would've been open to your encouragement at that in the moment, what is one thing you would have said?

3. Consider a time when you pulled away from God. What caused you to do so?

4. Using that one thing that you wrote about in question 2, write yourself a note of encouragement that could help you the next time you are tempted to pull away from God in a moment of frustration, misunderstanding, busyness, anger, or exhaustion.

5. Take a couple minutes to *lean in* to Him right now, through prayer, before going on with your day.

DAILY REFLECTION

Day 2

"Come near to God, and God will come near to you."

James 4:8a (ICB)

1. Read Psalm 145:18 and underline who the Lord is close to.

   "The Lord is close to all who call on him, yes, to all who call on him in truth."

   Psalm 145:18 (NLT)

2. Read these three verses below and circle the portion of each verse that describes who will be saved.

   "And everyone who calls on the name of the Lord will be saved."

   Joel 2:32a (NIV)

   "And everyone who calls on the name of the Lord will be saved."

   Acts 2:21 (NIV)

   "Everyone who calls on the name of the Lord will be saved."

   Romans 10:13b (NIV)

3. In the space provided, list the action steps given to the reader in each verse.

> "If you look for me wholeheartedly, you will find me."
>
> ***Jeremiah 29:13 (NLT)***

> "The name of the Lord is a strong fortress; the godly run to him and are safe."
>
> ***Proverbs 18:10 (NLT)***

There is a pattern throughout the Bible. When we *come close* to God we find Him. When we *call on* God we receive salvation, help, and hope. In each of these verses, we have an action step that *precedes* God's action step.

4. Write about a time where you got that order reversed—impatiently waiting for God to show up in your situation, but not taking the time to draw near to Him.

5. Now list a time when you got that order right—you came to God first and saw Him move in or through your situation.

God has given us free will, so while He desires to be a part of our daily lives, He waits for us to invite Him. Through Christ's death and resurrection, He already overcame all the barriers that separate us from His presence. Now the decision is ours. Do we include Him? Do we seek Him? Do we draw near? If we will, He promises to meet us.

DAILY REFLECTION

Day 3

"So let God work his will in you. Yell a loud *no* to the devil and watch him scamper. Say a quiet *yes* to God and he'll be there in no time."

James 4:8a (TM)

We were at this lovely, thin stretch of private beach at the foot of a massive cliff in Carlsbad, California one warm, overcast summer afternoon. It was serene, there was no one else around, and the tide was just starting to come in. My oldest son was about four years old at the time, and while his younger three-year-old brother loved the water, my oldest wasn't quite sure about it. He loved playing in the sand, though, and spent most of the day doing just that.

It was a small beach with a rock wall right behind us, and we had laid a sheet on the sand and placed all the toys on it. As the tide came up little by little, we scooted our sheet back until we were almost against the cliff face.

My husband had gone to rinse the sand off a few toys with our youngest son and I had just stepped a few yards away to grab something when a wave suddenly surged up all the way to our belongings and washed over the sheet. My four-year-old stood up, his back pressed against the rock wall, and let out a blood curdling scream! "JESUS, SAVE ME!" I stopped dead in my tracks, my heart pounding. I was alarmed at the panic I could hear echoed in that scream, but I was thrilled at *Who* he instinctively called upon for help. I will never forget the intensity of that little voice.

1. Explain what you tend to do when you feel up against a wall as a woman, wife, and/or mom.

2. Does your response typically include reaching out to God in some way? If so, what ways have you found to be effective? If not, point out why?

3. What word would you use to describe how often your kids ask you for something?

    - Frequently
    - Sometimes
    - Rarely
    - Never

Explain your answer.

4. What word would you use to describe how often *you* call on God throughout your day?

   Frequently
   Sometimes
   Rarely
   Never

Explain your answer.

5. Stop yourself in your tracks right now and call out to God. List below some of the areas where you long to see His saving grace at work in your life.

DAILY REFLECTION

Day 4

"Come close to the one true God, and He will draw close to you."

James 4:8a (THE VOICE)

1. In what ways have you fought against surrender?

2. To what do you equate "surrender?"

3. Now take a bit more time to think through surrender in light of what you've been learning this week. What can you equate it to with God's Word in mind?

4. Make a list of some things you can surrender to today that will help you come closer to God. Now give those to Him!

My list includes:

- My feelings of inadequacy.
- Time that I spend scrolling through social media in exchange for time spent catching up on my Bible reading plan.
- Giving up about 20 minutes of sleep in the morning so I can wake up before my kids and spend a few moments coming close to God
- My need for control. I surrender it daily, reminding myself that my greater need is to connect with God throughout my day. (Some days the reminder works, some days it doesn't, so I keep this on my list.)

5. In light of our weekly verse, finish this reminder to yourself by filling in the blanks: If I want God to draw closer to me, I need to _____________ ___________ _________ _________.

DAILY REFLECTION

Day 5—Wrap-Up

"Come close to God, and God will come close to you."

James 4:8a (NLT)

Sometimes God feels unreachable. We want to connect. We long to tune into His leading, but it feels unattainable. God has given us the power of choice while we live on this Earth. We do not have to choose Him. He has already chosen to love us. He has already pulled out all the stops to make it possible for us to have a relationship with Him. He stepped into our world as a baby. He died on the cross and took the punishment that sin demanded so that there was no longer any separation between God and us.

Now the decision is ours. Will we come? Will we step into relationship with Him daily or just in a crisis? Will we call on Him for strength and wisdom as we mother the children with which He has blessed us, or will we push through in our own strength, forgetting His offer and promise?

Like you, I want to be the best mom I can be, but the only way I can truly be my best is by coming close to God each and every day.

As we wrap-up this week, come close today. Thank Him for His ever-ready help. Pray and ask for all you need. Remind yourself that as you take the initiative to get closer to Him, you are allowing Him access into your life. You may not always feel like digging into the discipline it takes to build an ongoing relationship with

God but keep doing it anyway. Feelings are fickle, but God's Word is not. The outcome is worth the effort! When you draw near to God, He draws near to you.

Read God's Word

Over the next two days, I recommend you read James 4:1-10 and Psalms 145:13-21

#MOMLIFE DEVOTIONAL

Waiting

• **WEEK** SEVEN •

Week Seven

Are We There Yet?

"In the same way, the Holy Spirit helps us when we are weak. We don't know what we should pray for. But the Spirit himself prays for us. He prays through groans too deep for words. God, who looks into our hearts, knows the mind of the Spirit. And the Spirit prays for God's people just as God wants him to pray. We know that in all things God works for the good of those who love him. He appointed them to be saved in keeping with his purpose."

Romans 8:26-28 (NIRV)

"Are we there yet?" If you've ever gone on a long road trip (or even back and forth to church) with children, you've surely heard that question more times than needed. Yet have you ever asked that question yourself in frustration to God? It may not be "Are we there yet?" but something more along the lines of, "Are you hearing me?" "Do you see me, God?" "Do you know what's going on?" Perhaps it's, "How much longer *until* ... I'm married, I can get pregnant, the healing comes, my prodigal child returns home, or this relationship is fixed?" On and on our questions go, each one echoing the cry of our hearts.

Waiting is always difficult! Whether it's for the results of a medical test, an exciting package in the mail, that promised promotion to be finalized, your prayer to be answered, or your coffee to brew, it's never easy or desired.

I first wrote this devotional while sitting at my kitchen table and looking out the window at the "For Sale" sign planted like a flag in my front yard. It had been there for so long—four months—that it was starting to sprout cobwebs. It represented about 120 days of making sure my house was spotless and ready to be shown at any time. With four young sons, that in itself was enough to make me want to pull my hair out, strand by strand. Keeping up with the cleaning alone made me late almost everywhere I went.

Each day, I prayed for God to help us sell quickly and make the transition to our next home smooth. That was my hope—but never my reality. Instead, it was a lengthy, rough, emotional process—which I tended to overthink, adding to my sense of craziness. *Why isn't this home selling?* I'd lament. *Is it something we're doing? Is it our house? Is it the market? Is it just not God's timing? Is God trying to teach us a lesson through all this? Am I missing something?* On and on it went.

Well, the house didn't sell. We eventually found renters, and everything worked out. My anxiety did nothing to hasten the process, though—it just harried me. Through the waiting, I came to love how this week's verse says that the Holy Spirit prays for us with "groans too deep for words." When we are in times of waiting, questioning the why, the how long, and the future, sometimes the only thing we can get out is a groan. Frustration sinks in. Confusion clouds our thinking. Discouragement knocks at the door of our soul.

Then I recall how watching my mom slowly decline from cancer was one of those agonizing seasons filled with many sighs, "aching groans," and different kinds of waiting that were far more significant than the sale of our home. Waiting for a good day. Waiting at doctor's appointments. Waiting for different medications to kick in to relieve her pain. Some days I felt like I couldn't pray a single word. I just sat in my closet or my car with my heavy heart and simply sighed. My body and mind were tired. My emotions were fried. But God was still with me, surrounding me and offering His strength.

In both situations, the Lord was working behind the scenes—and He is still doing that in *all* of our moments of waiting and in all of our heavy seasons, creating beauty and weaving the loose threads of our lives into a beautiful tapestry. Even when it doesn't seem possible, He is the God who knows how to work everything together for our good. He redeems even the hardest times.

So take comfort in the waiting period. You may not be "there" yet, but God sees you right where you are.

Let's Pray:

Thank You, God, for working behind the scenes in my life. I choose to believe that since You can see the whole picture while I just see a part of it, I can look to You for guidance. Even in the times of waiting, Lord, I know You offer strength. Help me to continue leaning into that strength when I am feeling weak. You are a good God, and You are working Your good plan into even the messiest places of my heart and life. That You choose to be so close to me, to hear my sighs, is amazing. Continue leading my heart towards redemption and wholeness and daily dependence. In Jesus' Name, Amen.

DAILY REFLECTION

Day 1

> "Likewise the Spirit also helps in our weaknesses. For we do not know what we should pray for as we ought, but the Spirit Himself makes intercession for us with groanings which cannot be uttered. Now He who searches the hearts knows what the mind of the Spirit is, because He makes intercession for the saints according to the will of God. And we know that all things work together for good to those who love God, to those who are the called according to His purpose."
>
> ***Romans 8:26-28 (NKJV)***

1. Take a couple of moments to write about a heavy season, decision, or circumstance you are experiencing now or have recently gone through. Was there a time of waiting attached to it?

2. How have you held up in the wait?

3. How would you describe the nature of your prayers during this time?

4. In what ways did you know that God was still with you in the midst of what you were facing?

5. Take some time today to pray. Even if you are unable to muster any words, allow your heart to be open before God. Try journaling a few thoughts, feelings, and requests. You may not feel like they are the right words but get the ball rolling.

DAILY REFLECTION

Day 2

"In the same way, the Spirit helps us in our weakness. We do not know what we ought to pray for, but the Spirit himself intercedes for us through wordless groans. And he who searches our hearts knows the mind of the Spirit, because the Spirit intercedes for God's people in accordance with the will of God. And we know that in all things God works for the good of those who love him, who have been called according to his purpose."

Romans 8:26-28 (NIV)

1. As moms, we understand the work, effort, and preparation put in behind the scenes for our families to operate smoothly. We understand this because we are usually the ones doing most of it—the hours after the kids are in bed we spend on responsibilities such as making lunches, ironing, cleaning, laundry, catching up on bills, and sorting mail. Write about how your behind-the-scenes type of work relates to what our weekly passage of Scripture says that God does for us.

2. Consider a specific time when the Lord caused "everything to work together for good" in your life. Write about it here.

3. When you were at the beginning of this situation, could you see how it was all going to work out?

4. Knowing what you know now, how could you have handled things (even your own emotions) differently?

5. How can you help yourself carry the assurance that God is working with you, and behind the scenes on your behalf, into the next moment of uncertainty and waiting?

DAILY REFLECTION

Day 3

"Meanwhile, the moment we get tired in the waiting, God's Spirit is right alongside helping us along. If we don't know how or what to pray, it doesn't matter. He does our praying in and for us, making prayer out of our wordless sighs, our aching groans. He knows us far better than we know ourselves, knows our pregnant condition, and keeps us present before God. That's why we can be so sure that every detail in our lives of love for God is worked into something good."

Romans 8:26-28 (TM)

I know this translation isn't talking about a literal pregnancy, yet I have found myself in each of my four actual pregnancies needing the reminder that God knows my condition. For various reasons, I have walked through major transitions every time I was carrying my unborn sons. I'm not a big fan of change in the first place unless I'm initiating it, and I'm definitely less thrilled about it when I'm with child craving stability for my hormonal, emotional soul. I can think back on several instances where I sat crying, wondering how everything was going to turn out.

One transition experienced during pregnancy was especially difficult. We had an eight-month-old son when I found out I was two months along in pregnancy with our second child. We had recently learned that the ministry we were on staff with was relocating to a different state. Many of our coworkers and friends were excited for the move, but my husband and I knew we were supposed to stay where we were currently living. It not only meant saying goodbye to our closest friends and the ministry we loved so much, but also to our income and our insurance.

We knew God was calling us to stay in Arizona, but we didn't know what He was calling us to do. We knew we had a baby on the way and bills coming in each month, but we didn't know the next step yet. God knew, and He was going to soon lead us into a new season, but in those few months of uncertainty, job applications, prayer, and fasting, my fears, worries, and tears were never far away.

I'm so thankful that God not only understands the fact that we "get tired in the waiting," He makes provision for it! His Spirit is "right alongside helping us along." How comforting to know that the Holy Spirit sees our condition and keeps it present before the Father. "That's why we can be so sure that every detail in our lives of love for God is worked into something good."

1. How do you typically handle your waiting times?

2. In light of our passage of scripture this week, what are some ways you can become a better "waiter."

3. In what current situations do you need to be reminded (so that you can be sure) that the Holy Spirit knows your condition and is keeping it present before God?

4. Read Psalm 130:5 below and underline the last sentence in this verse.

> "I am counting on the Lord; yes, I am counting on him. I have put my hope in his word." Psalms 130:5 (NLT)

5. Before you end our time today, I encourage you to write out the last part of Psalm 130:5 that says, "I have put my hope in His Word." Let that be a reminder to you that there is always hope. It's found in Him.

DAILY REFLECTION

Day 4

"And the Holy Spirit helps us in our weakness. For example, we don't know what God wants us to pray for. But the Holy Spirit prays for us with groanings that cannot be expressed in words. And the Father who knows all hearts knows what the Spirit is saying, for the Spirit pleads for us believers in harmony with God's own will. And we know that God causes everything to work together for the good of those who love God and are called according to his purpose for them."

Romans 8:26-28 (NLT)

Let's break down verse 28.

1. *And we know...* Do you know? You may not know how or when or any of the details, but do you know that God's got this?

2. *...that God causes everything...* Yes, that says everything. It means the good and the bad, the health and the sickness, the provision and the lack, the success and the failure, the easy and the hard, the acceptance and the rejection, the changes, the frustrations, the joys, and everything in between.

3. *...to work together for the good...* God is weaving it all together. He is redeeming and readying us for good and greater things. He knows how to take the broken and make it whole. Nothing is impossible for God (Luke 1:37). He can create, re-create, heal, and restore. He does above and beyond what we can hope for (Ephesians 3:20).

4. *...of those who love God and are called according to his purpose for them.* Have you chosen to follow Christ? Do you love God? If so, my friend, this promise is for you! Whatever you are facing right now in your family, with your kids, in your home, on your job, *whatever*—know that God is working on your behalf for your good!

Be encouraged. This is God's Word to you!

5. Let's pray this passage of scripture over our lives today:

Father, thank You that the Holy Spirit helps me in my weakness. When I don't know what I should say or how I should pray, I'm relieved to know that the Holy Spirit prays for me in harmony with Your own will. Lord, I'm so grateful that You cause everything to work together for my good. I love You. In Jesus' Name, Amen.

DAILY REFLECTION

Day 5—Wrap Up

"In the same way, the Holy Spirit helps us when we are weak. We don't know what we should pray for. But the Spirit himself prays for us. He prays through groans too deep for words. God, who looks into our hearts, knows the mind of the Spirit. And the Spirit prays for God's people just as God wants him to pray. We know that in all things God works for the good of those who love him. He appointed them to be saved in keeping with his purpose."

Romans 8:26-28 (NIRV)

My hope for you is that Romans 8:26-28 will become your sounding board. When tough seasons come and when the waiting seems like it'll never end, I pray that you will know that God is at work on your behalf. When you don't feel Him, He is still there. When your patience wears thin, His strength will carry you through. When anxiety and fear begin to choke hope out of you, turn to His Word. By His grace, He redeems even our worst experiences.

He sees you right where you are. He knows how to get you to where you need to be. Trust His leading. Follow His Word. Rest in His ability. He is good, and His purpose for your life is, too!

Read God's Word

Over the next two days, I recommend you read Psalms 34:1-9 and Psalms 130:1-8

#MOMLIFE DEVOTIONAL

Through Christ

• WEEK EIGHT •

Week Eight

Can I?

"For I can do everything through Christ, who gives me strength."

Philippians 4:13 (NLT)

The studio was dark except for the neon light shining down on the instructor on the platform and the natural light being reflected in from the soothing indoor waterfall wall to our right. All of us in the packed space watched her climb onto her bike, place her feet onto the pedals, and take hold of the handlebars. We followed suit, readying ourselves for the workout to come.

Suddenly, the speakers pounded with Bon Jovi's *Livin' on a Prayer*, and I winced. I dislike rock, which turned out to be the only kind of music this cycling instructor played at her sessions. However, the one good thing about her genre choice was that I could tune it out and pray as I pedaled instead of distractedly singing along. It's the only aerobics class where I can actually pray while I exercise (multitasking strikes again), and truthfully, I *need* prayer to get myself through an hour-long cycling session.

On this particular day in class, a specific verse—Philippians 4:13—kept coming to mind, so I recited it through a couple of times thinking God was trying to encourage me with it. That would've been fine, but I was also praying through some hard emotions then, centered around a question I had been struggling with the past several months.

"What am I really good at?"

I was in the thick of ministry and motherhood, with so much going on most of the time that I easily doubted my effectiveness. I was constantly frustrated, doing a lot but wondering if was doing any of it *well.*

Second guessing yourself is exhausting. I know I'm not the only mom who's found that to be true. I wanted to find my niche, stay in my lane, soar with my strengths, and do it all with a smile! However, most days I was just struggling to keep up with my laundry and dishes while balancing my responsibilities at church.

I love being a mom and I love being in ministry. I believe God has called me to both, but I needed a better system. So as I pedaled and prayed, I felt the Lord lead me to replace the words "do everything" with *actual, specific* things in my life.

Here's just a dozen of the things I came up with as the sweat dripped down my face:

I can *be a great mom* through Christ, who gives me strength.
I can *lead my kids well* through Christ, who gives me strength.
I can *discipline them in love, not frustration,* through Christ, who gives me strength.
I can *be a loving, encouraging, steadfast, trusting, great wife* through Christ, who gives me strength.
I can *love others well* through Christ, who gives me strength.
I can *talk and connect with people (something I get insecure about often)* through Christ, who gives me strength.
I can *choose not to compare myself to others* through Christ, who gives me strength.
I can *write creatively and effectively* through Christ, who gives me strength.
I can *sense the Lord's leading* through Christ, who gives me strength.
I can *make wise decisions* through Christ, who gives me strength.
I can *be patient* through Christ, who gives me strength.
I can *walk in peace* through Christ, who gives me strength.

This week's verse is our reminder to replace our strength with *His*. We can default into operating out of our own ability and resources, forgetting we were never intended to live that way. We are meant to stay dependent on God because His strength never runs out, though ours definitely does. His wisdom, discernment, and peace are always available to us—so when we begin to doubt ourselves and wonder, "Can I?" His grace tells us, "You can as I strengthen you."

Now that's what I call livin' on a prayer!

Let's Pray:

Father, help me to remember daily that it's Your strength in which I am meant to live. You have not left me on my own. You see me and know all that is on my plate. Help me to take time each day to bring that plate to You. It's in seeking clarity from Your Spirit that I gain direction. Thank You for the all the blessings You've given me that have made my life full. Help me to remember to lean into Your grace so that I won't doubt myself or You. In Jesus' Name, Amen.

DAILY REFLECTION

Day 1

"I can do all things through Christ which strengtheneth me."
Philippians 4:13 (KJV)

1. What areas of your life are causing you to feel like you are coming up short?

2. Have you been operating in your own strength and wisdom in these areas?

3. Do you notice a difference in your life when you operate in your own ability instead of *living through Christ who strengthens you*? Explain your thoughts.

4. How consistent have you been in asking the Lord for His help?

5. Before you head out into the rest of you day, read this week's verse again like you believe it wholeheartedly!

DAILY REFLECTION

Day 2

"I can do all things through Christ who strengthens me."
Philippians 4:13 (NKJV)

1. Today, take some time to write out your own "I can" list, making sure to finish each statement with "through Christ, who gives me strength." Do a few, a dozen, or more.

2. Read over your list a few times and allow the truth of those statements to refresh your soul.

3. Can I challenge you to read through your "I can's" at least once a day for the next seven days? If you take me up on that challenge, write below (during this next week) how it helps you face and accomplish your responsibilities.

4. Find a place to keep your list where you can be reminded of it often.

5. Take a deep breath. Thank God for His presence in your life and step into your day knowing that *you can!*

DAILY REFLECTION

Day 3

"I can do all things [which He has called me to do] through Him who strengthens and empowers me [to fulfill His purpose—I am self-sufficient in Christ's sufficiency; I am ready for anything and equal to anything through Him who infuses me with inner strength and confident peace.]"

Philippians 4:13 (AMP)

We can't successfully manage everything on our plates in our own strength. Why? Because we were never meant to in the first place. God's plan has always been for us to lean into Him as He offers us His abundant resources. As we do, we flourish in a way that fulfills us and allows His purpose to overflow from our lives. Through Christ we are *enabled*. Dictionary.com defines the word "enabled" to mean: make able; give power or ability to; authorize.

Jesus makes us able! From His unlimited resources, He gives us the ability, competence, and means to do what He has purposed us to do. But so often we just go, go, go until we wear out. Only then (it seems) in our exasperation do we call out to the Lord. What if we stopped living that way? I venture to say that we'll start *thriving* instead of just surviving.

We can choose to consistently live our lives through Christ's enablement and through His infusion of inner strength and competent peace—so lean in today. Your Heavenly Father has got your back!

1. In your own words, explain how life looks when you operate in your own strength until you come to the end of your rope *and then* ask God for help versus asking for His guidance first and all along the way. (Then circle which way you tend to live.)

2. Describe how consistency is needed to help you live more connected to Christ.

3. Picture yourself leaning in to God today—really relaxing in His presence, knowing that He has you (and everything you will face) already covered.

4. What are some things (possibly even current trials or struggles) that you know the Spirit of God will enable you to navigate through as you allow Him to infuse you with inner strength and confident peace?

5. Read through your "I can" list again today. Speak each one over yourself in truth, boldness, and encouragement.

DAILY REFLECTION

Day 4

"Christ gives me the strength to face anything."

Philippians 4:13 (CEV)

1. Read the passage below which includes the scriptures preceding our verse for the week:

> "How I praise the Lord that you are concerned about me again. I know you have always been concerned for me, but you didn't have the chance to help me. Not that I was ever in need, for I have learned how to be content with whatever I have. I know how to live on almost nothing or with everything. I have learned the secret of living in every situation, whether it is with a full stomach or empty, with plenty or little. For I can do everything through Christ, who gives me strength."
>
> ***Philippians 4:10-13 (NLT)***

You have written your "I can" list, but let's focus today on verse 11:

> "Not that I was ever in need, for I have learned how to be content with whatever I have."

Part of feeling fulfilled rather than frustrated is knowing how to be content. Just as it is *through Christ* that we can do all things, it is also *through Christ* that we learn contentment. The two go together. Paul is saying in verse 11 that he learned to be content—and because of his contentment, he can trust God to equip him to accomplish all that he needs to do.

2. When we are worried and anxious, we strive. When we trust God, we are content, knowing that He is the sufficient one. That trust enables us to be equipped with whatever we may face. Explain how you have seen these principles unfold in your own life.

3. Many times we second guess ourselves because we are trying to control things in our own strength instead of contentedly trusting in God's strength and timing. In what ways has discontentment crept in and added to your feelings of inadequacy? List them below.

4. How have you seen contentment impact your thoughts, attitude, and relationships?

5. Take a few moments today to pray and ask God to help you to trust Him right where you're at with what you have.

DAILY REFLECTION

Day 5—Wrap-Up

"For I can do everything through Christ, who gives me strength."

Philippians 4:13 (NLT)

I pray this verse has been a powerful reminder for you this week—like pushing the refresh button for the soul. We don't have to figure out a way to do it all and be everything to everyone!

Often, we just need to change the way we think and speak about ourselves. Where the enemy of your soul has crept in to undermine your faith through negativity and fear, begin to speak life and truth by declaring God's Word over yourself and your situation!

You might not be able to accomplish what you want on your own, but you can do all things through Christ. While there are many areas where you *can* succeed in your own strength, you will do them *better* and with greater purpose through connecting to Christ's unlimited resources.

If what you believe about yourself and your situation doesn't line up with God's Word, declare this verse boldly and often. Your strength, ability, success, and fulfillment are found *in* and *through* Christ. This truth will challenge you to intentionally stay in tune with Him throughout your day, reminding yourself to swap ME for HE.

You *can* flourish in this *#MOMLIFE* through Christ who gives you strength!

Read God's Word

Over the next two days, I recommend you read Colossians 1:9-13 and Philippians 4:4-13.

#MOMLIFE DEVOTIONAL

Well Rounded

• **WEEK** NINE •

Week Nine

A Sigh of Relief

"Consider it a sheer gift, friends, when tests and challenges come at you from all sides. You know that under pressure, your faith-life is forced into the open and shows its true colors. So don't try to get out of anything prematurely. Let it do its work so you become mature and well-developed, not deficient in any way. If you don't know what you're doing, pray to the Father. He loves to help. You'll get his help and won't be condescended to when you ask for it. Ask boldly, believingly, without a second thought. People who 'worry their prayers' are like wind-whipped waves. Don't think you're going to get anything from the Master that way, adrift at sea, keeping all your options open."

James 1:2-8 (TM)

The sun was shining, the breeze was warm, and my arms were tired. My baby boy was still in his car seat carrier, and I had to hold him in it because there wasn't a single available space left on the benches at the park. Everyone was there—my husband, all four of our boys, and two of my nieces—and since it was spring break, the playground area was teeming with children.

My arms were still aching when my husband offered to go get some pizzas at the restaurant across the street. My stomach rumbled at the thought of food, and I hoped to find a picnic table nearby so that I could put my baby son down.

As he left for the parking lot, the five remaining kids scattered in all directions to get a few more minutes on the four jungle gym structures within my view. When he returned, I got up and started calling everyone to come together. Child after child showed up—except for our three-year-old. He wasn't there. I was nearly certain I had caught a glimpse of him just moments before, but now he was nowhere to be seen.

My husband quickly took the car seat carrier and we started walking and calling. Then I started shouting. Panicking. I ran over to the nearby lake, shouting his name. Nothing. I backtracked toward the parking lot, suddenly dizzy as my adrenaline spiked.

That's when I saw them—a couple coming from across the lot, leading my son by the hand. I ran over, bent down, and took him in my arms. Tears filled my eyes as I squeezed him, relieved that none of my worst fears had come true. I thanked the couple profusely while feeling embarrassed at the same time to have obviously lost track of my child.

It wasn't like him to wander off, but it was like him to want to be with daddy. He apparently had tried to follow his father, wanting to go with him to get pizza. When he couldn't find him, he just kept walking across the busy parking lot, winding up at the skate park filled with teenagers. Moments later, as everyone was eating pizza, I thanked God out loud for His protection over my son. Then I hugged my little guy once more, again breathing a massive sigh of relief.

Sometimes I can feel so weighed down by the stresses and worries of life. On days like that, it's easy for me to forget God is there, looking out for me. Yet when I do, everything only gets more overwhelming. My messes are magnified. My shortcomings stand out. Anxiety sets in.

Sometimes our spiritual vision gets blurry and we aren't able to see how God is using all we are experiencing to mature us into well-rounded daughters and mamas. The Lord is developing our character, and when we are at a loss about how to handle it all—everything from piles of laundry to our messy hair, or even a temporarily missing child—God offers His wisdom.

"If you don't know what you're doing, pray to the Father," this week's passage reads in verse 5. "He loves to help. You'll get His help and won't be condescended to when you ask for it." I love that! Doesn't it make you want to let out a big sigh of relief?

I liken it to going to your child's yearly check-up at the pediatrician. You get a chance to ask if the behaviors and issues you're observing are a normal part of his or her development. If you're anything like me, you've already come up with a variety of diagnoses for your child's peculiarities, some of them negative or worse. But when you hear the reminder from the doctor that your son or daughter is still developing and will outgrow most of the concerns you may have, it brings relief.

Guess what? We are still developing spiritually, too! No matter how old we get, there will still be growing pains from the challenges or fears we encounter. This week's passage tells us that it's all a normal part of our development.

So be relieved. You are not unseen by God. Don't give in to a living a life of worry. He has not forgotten you or how to fulfill His promises in you. Let's take James up on his suggestion and start asking God for His wisdom in our lives today.

Let's Pray:

God, there is so much going on in my life. Please help me to look to You instead of getting overwhelmed. I trust that You are working in ways I cannot see, and I ask You to continue shaping me to be the woman You have created me to be. I want to continue growing, and yet sometimes I balk at the things that bring maturity into my life. Thank You for offering Your wisdom. I need it every day, so today Lord, I ask for it. Help me to know the best choices to make as I face whatever comes my way this day. Enable me to stay in tune with Your leading even when my life gets busy or scary. In Jesus' Name, Amen.

DAILY REFLECTION

Day 1

"Dear brothers and sisters, when troubles of any kind come your way, consider it an opportunity for great joy. For you know that when your faith is tested, your endurance has a chance to grow. So let it grow, for when your endurance is fully developed, you will be perfect and complete, needing nothing. If you need wisdom, ask our generous God, and he will give it to you. He will not rebuke you for asking. But when you ask him, be sure that your faith is in God alone. Do not waver, for a person with divided loyalty is as unsettled as a wave of the sea that is blown and tossed by the wind. Such people should not expect to receive anything from the Lord. Their loyalty is divided between God and the world, and they are unstable in everything they do."

James 1:2-8 (NLT)

1. Write down what sticks out to you most in these verses.

2. What tests and challenges are you currently facing with your children?

3. Have you stopped to consider these trials an opportunity for you (and your kids) to grow? If not, do so now and write down at least one way you can potentially see growth being the outcome.

4. Fill in the blanks from verses 2-4 of our weekly passage listed above.

> "Dear brothers and sisters, when troubles of any kind come your way, consider it an opportunity for__________. For you know that when your ____________ is tested, your ______________ has a chance to grow. So _____________ grow, for when your endurance is _______________, you will be perfect and ______________, needing nothing."

5. How do these three verses challenge you and your faith walk?

DAILY REFLECTION

Day 2

"Dear brothers, is your life full of difficulties and temptations? Then be happy, for when the way is rough, your patience has a chance to grow. So let it grow, and don't try to squirm out of your problems. For when your patience is finally in full bloom, then you will be ready for anything, strong in character, full and complete. If you want to know what God wants you to do, ask him, and he will gladly tell you, for he is always ready to give a bountiful supply of wisdom to all who ask him; he will not resent it. But when you ask him, be sure that you really expect him to tell you, for a doubtful mind will be as unsettled as a wave of the sea that is driven and tossed by the wind; and every decision you then make will be uncertain, as you turn first this way and then that. If you don't ask with faith, don't expect the Lord to give you any solid answer."

James 1:2-8 translation (TLB)

1. Have you prematurely tried to squirm your way out of your problems and challenges? What was the outcome?

2. Now think about how a challenging experience has impacted your character development. Use the space below to write about it.

3. It's typically difficult to feel joy in the midst of unpleasant moments, but can you recall a time you felt joy over the spiritual growth and maturity you saw blossoming in your life?

4. Take a moment and thank God for the progress He brought through that experience.

5. Verse 4 ends by listing three things that will happen once your patience is "finally in full bloom." List those things below.

   - Then you will be ready __________ __________,
   - strong in __________,
   - full and __________.

DAILY REFLECTION

Day 3

> "My brethren, count it all joy when you fall into various trials, knowing that the testing of your faith produces patience. But let patience have its perfect work, that you may be perfect and complete, lacking nothing. If any of you lacks wisdom, let him ask of God, who gives to all liberally and without reproach, and it will be given to him. But let him ask in faith, with no doubting, for he who doubts is like a wave of the sea driven and tossed by the wind. For let not that man suppose that he will receive anything from the Lord; he is a double-minded man, unstable in all his ways."
>
> ***James 1:2-8 (NKJV)***

This is a prayer I wrote in my journal during a difficult season.

> "Lord, this year has continued to prove challenging. Help me navigate through the painful situations in a way that honors you with wisdom, grace, truth, and love. Teach me through this process, Lord, what you would have me to learn. Continue leading me to be more like you, pruning, shaping, and molding my life. It's uncomfortable right now, but I surrender through it. My life is yours and I trust you."

Typically, when I am going through a hard time and find myself unsure how to proceed, worry is right there, clouding my thoughts. When that happens one of my favorite verses to turn to is 1 John 3:20b.

> "For God is greater than our worried hearts and knows more about us than we do ourselves." (The Message)

No matter what adversities we face, the truth is that God is greater, and He knows how to help us. He knows our minds are prone to worry. In Matthew, Jesus taught on worry and encouraged His listeners by saying:

> "That is why I tell you not to worry about everyday life—whether you have enough food and drink, or enough clothes to wear. Isn't life more than food, and your body more than clothing? ... Can all your worries add a single moment to your life?"
>
> ***Matthew 6:25, 27 (NLT)***

What good does worry do us? None. It's never helpful. God tells us not to worry and instead invites us to ask Him for wisdom. We may not know what to do or how things will turn out, but He does. When life's challenges come our way, we can choose to worry or seek His wisdom.

Our weekly passage reminds us that the trials we encounter are not for nothing. They are producing patience and wholeness in our lives. There is purpose amidst the pain. The more we trust God through the trials, the more we become the well-rounded mamas He is shaping us to be.

1. List at least one area (or a few) in your life right now in which you lack wisdom to know what to do or how to best proceed.

2. When those feelings of inadequacy and/or confusion arise, is worry or fear a typical response?

3. Write down some of your worries.

4. Is it hard for you to believe that God will give you the wisdom you need? Why or why not?

5. Spend some time in prayer surrendering your list of worries to God and asking for His wisdom. I encourage you to pray with faith and believe that the Lord is at work in your life.

DAILY REFLECTION

Day 4

"Don't run from tests and hardships, brothers and sisters. As difficult as they are, you will ultimately find joy in them; if you embrace them, your faith will blossom under pressure and teach you true patience as you endure. And true patience brought on by endurance will equip you to complete the long journey and cross the finish line—mature, complete, and wanting nothing. If you don't have all the wisdom needed for this journey, then all you have to do is ask God for it; and God will grant all that you need. He gives lavishly and never scolds you for asking. The key is that your request be anchored by your single-minded commitment to God. Those who depend only on their own judgment are like those lost on the seas, carried away by any wave or picked up by any wind. Those adrift on their own wisdom shouldn't assume the Lord will rescue them or bring them anything. The splinter of divided loyalty shatters your compass and leaves you dizzy and confused."

James 1:2-8 (THE VOICE)

1. Read the following verses:

   "For the Lord grants wisdom! From his mouth come knowledge and understanding."

   Proverbs 2:6 (NLT)

   "How much better to get wisdom than gold, and good judgment than silver!"

   Proverbs 16:16 (NLT)

"To acquire wisdom is to love yourself; people who cherish understanding will prosper."

Proverbs 19:8 (NLT)

2. How do these verses, in conjunction with James 1:5, speak to your heart?

3. Are you currently putting as much value on acquiring wisdom as the Word of God does? If not, what can you begin doing to ensure that it becomes your pursuit?

4. Circle which descriptive word James 1:5 uses when explaining how God will give wisdom when we ask. *Rarely. Lavishly. Sparingly.* Does knowing this truth cause you to want to ask Him for wisdom more often than you currently do?

5. His Word *encourages* you to ask, *confirms* His desire to help, and *challenges* you to believe that He will. With this in mind, write out a prayer today asking God for wisdom in specific areas of your life.

I pray that seeking *God's wisdom* will become a daily habit for you!

DAILY REFLECTION

Day 5—Wrap Up

"Consider it a sheer gift, friends, when tests and challenges come at you from all sides. You know that under pressure, your faith-life is forced into the open and shows its true colors. So don't try to get out of anything prematurely. Let it do its work so you become mature and well-developed, not deficient in any way. If you don't know what you're doing, pray to the Father. He loves to help. You'll get his help, and won't be condescended to when you ask for it. Ask boldly, believingly, without a second thought. People who 'worry their prayers' are like wind-whipped waves. Don't think you're going to get anything from the Master that way, adrift at sea, keeping all your options open."

James 1:2-8 (TM)

As moms, it's often hard to know if we are doing the right thing. We can question and second guess our decisions as we try to look ahead to see the implications they may or may not carry on our children. There are so many opinions, parenting styles, and pressures all around us in our society today, and all those can add up to one, big, heavy burden a mom carries around.

God never intended us to live the *#MOMLIFE* by ourselves. This week's passage of scripture is one we need to remind ourselves of often. When we don't know the right thing to do, words to say, place to go, or decision to make, we can lean into our Heavenly Father and seek His wisdom.

Remember, the Lord sees the big picture. He knows how to help us be successful women, wives, moms, friends, and daughters—and in His faithfulness, He pours out His wisdom on those who seek it. Let's not be the moms who go through life guilt-ridden and full of worry and fear. Instead, let's be the ones who seek His wisdom so that we can freely and confidently walk in it!

Read God's Word

Over the next two days, I recommend you read 1 Peter 1:3-9 and Proverbs 3:1-8

#MOMLIFE DEVOTIONAL

Lean In

• **WEEK** TEN •

Week Ten

I Don't Know How

"The Lord your God in your midst, The Mighty One, will save; He will rejoice over you with gladness, He will quiet *you* with His love, He will rejoice over you with singing."

Zephaniah 3:17 (NKJV)

Kindergarten took my third-born son by storm—and the rest of the family got swept up in it.

It was the hardest school transition that we ever went through with one of our kids. There were tears and hesitation with his two older brothers when they started school, but neither one was nearly as traumatic. It shouldn't have surprised me, though. My third-born has always been the most passionate one of the brothers.

He shed *lots* of tears. Just the thought of going back to school made him weep. He cried as he was getting ready in the morning. He sobbed as he stood among his classmates through the Pledge of Allegiance and God Bless America. Neither his friends, his cool shoes, nor even his Star Wars backpack were enough consolation. When he got home, he was always testy, constantly on edge.

I wish I could say I glided effortlessly through that hectic time with ease and grace, but that's just not the truth. It was more like bumping and banging my way through it. As I was blown to and fro by the storm of a very loud and passionately disgruntled child, along with the busyness of everyday life, frustration and stress set the atmosphere in my household. I knew the chaos was going on around me, but I couldn't figure out how to stop it.

Then came the day the storm made landfall. I was in the kitchen making dinner and I could hear his brothers pushing his buttons as only they could. I couldn't hear what they were saying, and before I could get in there to figure it out, my third-born firecracker went off! He became a whirlwind of angry words, nasty attitude, and raw emotion—and he wouldn't be calmed.

"You're gonna go sit in time out," I warned. "You're gonna get in trouble!" By the time I got into the room, he was all over his brothers—hitting, pushing, and wrestling. By then, he was hysterical. I pulled him off the boys and sent him up to his room.

I figured I'd let him get all his tears out and he'd calm down—until he started pounding on the floor with his fists and kicking the wall with his heels, behavior he knew I didn't tolerate. I went up to his room and looked down at him throwing his wild fit on the floor.

"You *better* stop!" I scolded, ready for him to fight me on that. But I wasn't prepared for what he said next.

"I can't stop!" he yelled brokenly, tears streaming down his cheeks. "I don't know how."

Usually when my kids throw tantrums, a "nails on the chalkboard" kind of alarm goes off inside of me. My body gets tense and my blood pressure soars. This time, though, was different. Maybe it was his big brown eyes looking so helpless, or perhaps it was because *I* had been feeling like life was out of control. It could've been a nudge from the Lord. Whatever the catalyst, in that moment of his honest confession, my heart melted. I sat down beside him, swooped him up onto my lap, grabbed a book, and started reading. Two lines into the story, I felt his entire body relax as he leaned back against me. His tension was gone, his sobbing subsided.

When the book was done, we had an honest conversation. He apologized, I held him, and we both felt better.

Then I realized it. I had been *feeling* the same way he had been *acting*. I was frustrated and emotional. I felt stuck. I wanted to be handling things more successfully, but I wasn't. I felt like I just didn't know how. In his little five-year-old voice, he said the same words my own heart had been saying for months.

I'm still always amazed when I learn such big lessons from my little guys. When life gets stressful and chaotic, when things turn out differently than I expected, and when I'm convinced there's not enough of me to go around, I need to lean into the strength that my Heavenly Father offers. He's always there to step in and graciously swoop me up into His loving presence—but sometimes I'm so busy throwing a fit, I fail to recognize that.

This week's verse tells us we have a God who knows how to help us. He knows how to quiet our minds and hearts when life is spinning all around us. He knows how to hold us and love us better than even the best earthly parent. His grace will steady us in the storm and get us back on the right track.

Let's Pray:

Father, today I choose to lean into You. I can't control all that's going on around me. Frustration and anxiety want to make themselves at home within me, but I choose to allow Your Word to speak over me. I need to remember that You are always there, ready for me to call upon You for help, strength, and wisdom. Forgive me for the times I've just thrown a tantrum and pulled away from You in confusion and hurt. Right now, I come to You, and I ask for Your guidance. Thank you for surrounding me with Your love, even now. In Jesus' Name, Amen.

DAILY REFLECTION

Day 1

"For the Lord your God is living among you. He is a mighty savior. He will take delight in you with gladness. With his love, he will calm all your fears. He will rejoice over you with joyful songs."

Zephaniah 3:17 (NLT)

Let's dissect this verse a bit together to help us really grasp what it's saying.

1. Who does this verse say that God is?

2. Where does this verse say that God is?

3. What three things will God do for us?

4. What will He do those three things *with*?

5. How does that speak to your heart today?

DAILY REFLECTION

Day 2

"The Lord your God is with you, the Mighty Warrior who saves. He will take great delight in you; in his love he will no longer rebuke you but will rejoice over you with singing."

Zephaniah 3:17 (NIV)

1. Are there any areas of your life right now where you feel stuck, not sure how to move forward? If so, how are you navigating through them?

2. How can this verse be a source of steadfastness for your emotions?

3. Write down a phrase from Zephaniah 3:17 that encourages you the most right now.

4. As our arms wrap around our children, allow that phrase today to wrap around your heart and mind as you meditate on it.

5. Ask God to reveal His nearness to you today.

DAILY REFLECTION

Day 3

> "The Lord your God is among you; He is mighty to save. He will rejoice over you with gladness; He will quiet you with His love; He will rejoice over you with singing."
>
> ***Zephaniah 3:17 (BSB)***

My boys almost always want me to sing to them at night. I am not a singer, but I *love* that they like my singing. I enjoy pulling them in close, wrapping my arms around them, and watching them quiet down and get ready to sleep as I sing. As parents, we just *do* things like this for our sons and daughters.

Can you sit for a few moments right now envisioning your Heavenly Father singing over you? What an amazing concept. When your mind is racing, your thoughts jumbled, or your heart heavy, picture the truths in this verse taking place in the spiritual realm. When circumstances are messy, speak these words over your anxious soul. The outcome ahead may be beyond your control and fear might be rising, but the truth of God's Word never changes. No matter what noisy chaos is going on around you, your God *will quiet you with His love and rejoice over you with singing*.

1. As a mom, have you ever done of any of the things listed in this verse for your own children? If so, write about how you have.

2. How do your kids react when you engage with them this way?

3. Take a moment to visually picture yourself as the daughter and God as your Heavenly Father. Write down how it makes you feel to envision Him "rejoicing over you with singing and gladness and quieting you with His love."

4. What areas of your heart need to be quieted with God's love today?

5. Take some time to be still before Almighty God and allow His love to refresh you right now.

DAILY REFLECTION

Day 4

"The Lord your God is with you. The mighty One will save you. The Lord will be happy with you. You will rest in his love. He will sing and be joyful about you."

Zephaniah 3:17 (ICB)

1. Today's translation says, "The Lord will be happy with you." Is it easy or difficult for you to believe that God is happy with you? Explain your answer.

2. Below, write out the verse in first person—as if you were reading this verse to yourself.

3. Now read it out loud the way you just wrote it down.

4. How could your *daily* life change for the better if you would think about the fact that the Lord Almighty is in your midst rejoicing over you and loving you each day?

5. Write yourself a note encouraging your heart to be at rest in the Father's love today. Use specific situations you may be currently facing to remind yourself that He is with you amidst it all—calming you, giving you peace, and celebrating His love for you.

DAILY REFLECTION

Day 5—Wrap-Up

"The Lord your God in your midst, The Mighty One, will save; He will rejoice over you with gladness, He will quiet *you* with His love, He will rejoice over you with singing."

Zephaniah 3:17 (NKJV)

I'm not sure how this week has gone for you. Perhaps you've faced disappointment, heartache, frustration, or a lack of support. Maybe you've had a full schedule and are simply worn out. Or it could be your week has been smooth and beautiful, and if so, I rejoice with you! Whatever it has looked like, my hope and prayer is that Zephaniah 3:17 has become a part of your daily thought process this week.

This verse paints a picture that will help carry us through so many moments and seasons in our lives. In everything we face, God is still good. His love still surrounds us. His grace still steadies our shakiness. He is our loving Heavenly Father and delights in us as His daughters, even when we're a mess. Whew!

Continue to meditate on this verse, allowing the Lord God to minister to your heart through it.

You are loved.
You are seen.
You are cherished.

Read God's Word

Over the next two days, I recommend you read Psalms 136:1-9 and 1 John 4:13-19.

#MOMLIFE DEVOTIONAL

Stay Connected

• **WEEK** ELEVEN •

Week Eleven

Ice Cream and A Good Cry

"Remain in me, and I will remain in you. For a branch cannot produce fruit if it is severed from the vine, and you cannot be fruitful unless you remain in me. Yes, I am the vine; you are the branches. Those who remain in me, and I in them, will produce much fruit. For apart from me you can do nothing."

John 15:4-5 (NLT)

Let's talk about meltdowns. They're frustrating, intense, and embarrassing. Oh, and they're like that when my kids have them, too—but right now I'm talking about my own. I know I'm not the only one, right?

One such meltdown came on a hot summer evening. Where I live, it's still about 110 degrees *after* the sun has gone done, which means three things. First, it's hot! Second, since all four of my boys have been home all day because school is out, they're hot. Third, when they're hot, they get whiny and irritated, which means they tattle and argue. And when they tattle and argue, my patience flies right out the window.

Throughout the day, the boys had been fighting with each other. Even after I got them out of the house to break the day up a bit, they kept quarreling back and forth with each other. This led to more tattling. My husband has a way of tuning it out, but not me.

So that evening, he was out playing basketball with some friends, and I was getting the boys ready for bed. Doing that when your patience is thin is never a good idea. I sat myself in the yellow rocking chair in the baby's room trying to rock him to sleep—and the boys, one by one, kept coming into the room, asking silly questions or saying silly things in their silly attempt to stay up when they *knew* they should've been staying in bed. Even worse, every time one of them came in, the baby lifted his head, becoming more awake and alert each time. This caused me to become more irritated with each interruption.

All at once, the chaos from the day caught up with me—and I lost it. I told my kids to get in bed and *stay* there. I was exhausted, but no one seemed to want to go to sleep except me. I tried calming the baby down while unsuccessfully trying to calm my emotions. I could feel tears pricking my eyes as all the frustration from the day came surging to the forefront of my mind.

Before I knew it, I broke down. It wasn't a throwing-things-and-yelling kind of tantrum. It was a crying-my-eyes-out mama meltdown, the kind where every little thing that is *kind of* bugging you seems a hundred times more magnified. The type of emotional overload where you feel like a failure at everything, and you wish you could just do more and *be* more.

I kept myself as quiet as possible so that the baby could go to sleep but sobs literally shook my shoulders for several minutes as the emotions poured out from me. Eventually, I started to calm down, and I reminded myself again what I knew to be true: God hadn't left me to do this *#MOMLIFE* thing on my own. Many days I feel like I'm not enough, and the truth is, I'm not. I wasn't meant to be enough by myself. In this week's Bible passage, Jesus teaches the disciples that they needed to remain connected to Him if they wanted to be successful. He told them that apart from that connection, they couldn't do anything worthwhile. That didn't de-value them—or us. It actually increases our value! We were always intended to enlist God's help in our daily lives, not just in an emotional crisis, when the heat is on, or when we're falling apart in a yellow rocking chair.

So where did the ice cream come in? After the meltdown, of course. When all my boys were finally asleep, and my tears had dried, I enjoyed a bit of my favorite, mint chocolate chip, in quiet solitude. There's just something about a good cry and some ice cream that seems to help put things back into perspective. I know I'm not alone on that one, either.

My pastor recently said, "A breakdown often leads to a breakthrough." It did for me that night. In those moments when I'm a hot mess because it's 110 degrees outside and I have four non-stop, energetic boys, I'm thankful for God's loving reminder that tempers my emotions: He is the Vine, and my success comes from staying connected to Him.

Let's Pray:

Father, help me to stay connected to You daily. When my heart is prone to wander, lead me back to You. When my pride creeps in, pushing me to do things on my own, lead me back to You. My connection to You is vital. Help my spirit to remember that throughout my day. I want to live in the overflow of my relationship with You. You are the supplier of all I need. Thank You, Lord. In Jesus' Name, Amen.

DAILY REFLECTION

Day 1

"Remain in me, and I in you. Just as a branch is unable to produce fruit by itself unless it remains on the vine, neither can you unless you remain in me. I am the vine; you are the branches. The one who remains in me and I in him produces much fruit, because you can do nothing without me."

John 15:4-5 translation (CSB)

1. Have you had a meltdown or near meltdown lately? If so, write about it.

2. How do you tend to compensate for those feelings that lead to emotional exhaustion?

3. What does this passage say is the key for producing fruit in our lives?

4. How does being connected to the Lord help you accomplish things?

5. List three practical ways you can *remain* in Christ this week.

DAILY REFLECTION

Day 2

"Remain in me, and I will remain in you. A branch cannot produce fruit alone but must remain in the vine. In the same way, you cannot produce fruit alone but must remain in me. I am the vine, and you are the branches. If any remain in me and I remain in them, they produce much fruit. But without me they can do nothing."

John 15:4-5 (NCV)

1. Read the next five verses of this week's passage:

"If any do not remain in me, they are like a branch that is thrown away and then dies. People pick up dead branches, throw them into the fire, and burn them. If you remain in me and follow my teachings, you can ask anything you want, and it will be given to you.

You should produce much fruit and show that you are my followers, which brings glory to my Father. I loved you as the Father loved me. Now remain in my love. I have obeyed my Father's commands, and I remain in his love. In the same way, if you obey my commands, you will remain in my love. I have told you these things so that you can have the same joy I have and so that your joy will be the fullest possible joy."

John 15:6-11 (NCV)

2. How many times do you see the word *remain* listed in verses 4-10?

3. Take a couple of minutes and write out what Jesus said each time He mentioned the directive to "remain" in these verses.

    - Verse 4:
    - Verse 5:
    - Verse 6:
    - Verse 7:
    - Verse 9:
    - Verse 10:

4. In verse 11, what does Jesus say is produced in the life of one who follows the principles lined out in the previous verses?

5. From this passage, summarize in your own words the benefits of staying connected to Jesus and the danger of becoming disconnected.

Reflect on this today.

DAILY REFLECTION

Day 3

"Remain in Me, and I [will remain] in you. Just as no branch can bear fruit by itself without remaining in the vine, neither can you [bear fruit, producing evidence of your faith] unless you remain in Me. I am the Vine; you are the branches. The one who remains in Me and I in him bears much fruit, for [otherwise] apart from Me [that is, cut off from vital union with Me] you can do nothing."

John 15:4-5 (AMP)

My oldest son is constantly bossing around his younger siblings. I find myself continuously reminding him that his role in our family is not that of the parent. I want to relieve him of the pressure of trying to carry that load. "Parenting is for dad and me," I say. Yet often I still hear him slipping into that role reversal.

The truth is I often get my role mixed up, too. In the same way my son tries to take on my responsibilities, I can tend to attempt taking on God's. I don't know about you, but I have been guilty plenty of times of running around trying to be everyone's Vine. I've felt overwhelmed more times than I can count by trying so hard to "nourish" all those around me. When I realized that's not my role, I threw up my hands and thanked the Lord!

Our role is to live in connection to the Vine. In nature, the vine sustains the branches. Then, as the plant grows in a healthy state, fruit is produced. Spiritually speaking, God is the One who nourishes and fills us. *Out of that connection*, we bear fruit which can then bless others. This was God's design.

Apart from God we come up short, but with God, we thrive! We become the women we want to be—the women God created us to be. Strong. Refreshed. Life givers. Purposeful. Grace filled.

I hope that refreshes you today! It sure lightens *my* heart.

1. Do you sometimes find yourself mixing up your roles, striving and struggling to be the Vine in your life and relationships? Explain your answer.

2. How do you typically feel when you try to do the job of the Vine instead of the job of the branch?

3. In what ways do you find yourself lacking when you operate apart from God?

4. How does knowing your true role bring freedom?

5. List one area of "fruit" that you have seen in your own life when you have chosen to *remain in Christ*.

DAILY REFLECTION

Day 4

"Live in me. Make your home in me just as I do in you. In the same way that a branch can't bear grapes by itself but only by being joined to the vine, you can't bear fruit unless you are joined with me. I am the Vine, you are the branches. When you're joined with me and I with you, the relation intimate and organic, the harvest is sure to be abundant. Separated, you can't produce a thing."

John 15:4-5 (TM)

1. Write out the weekly passage, John 15:4-5, in your favorite translation.

2. On a scale of 1-10, 1 being the least and 10 being the most, rate how often you take on the job of the Vine.

3. On a scale of 1-10, 1 being the least and 10 being the most, rate how often you disconnect from the Vine throughout your week.

4. On a scale of 1-10, 1 being the least and 10 being the most, how much fruit do you feel you are producing in your life?

5. Take a few minutes to set some practical goals that will help you get the numbers on those scales closer to where you would like them to be. For example:

    1. I can choose to live more like the branch rather than the Vine by ____________________
    2. I can connect throughout my day/week to the Vine by________ __________________________________
    3. I will see more fruit growing in my life when ______________________ _____________________________________

DAILY REFLECTION

Day 5—Wrap-Up

"Remain in me, and I will remain in you. For a branch cannot produce fruit if it is severed from the vine, and you cannot be fruitful unless you remain in me. Yes, I am the vine; you are the branches. Those who remain in me, and I in them, will produce much fruit. For apart from me you can do nothing."

John 15:4-5 (NLT)

Jesus directs us to stay in close connection with Him throughout our lives. He gives us the benefits of doing so, and He also lays out the dangers of refusing to live this way. It can sound harsh, yet He explains how it's for our benefit. When we remain in Him by living in close relationship with Him, we are filled with both His love and overflowing joy. In this passage, He teaches us how to fully live in the abundance of life He has for us.

We miss out on this so often because we disconnect. We try to operate in our own strength, yet we all know that at some point that wears out.

God has designed a better way for us to live. His way never leaves us empty and dry. As we live in connection with Him, He continually fills us. Out of that filling, we bear fruit. Then our fruit can bless our families, our kids, our friends, and everyone else in our sphere of life. It brings success, fulfillment, and enjoyment. However, don't miss this: the fruit doesn't come *unless* you are connected to the Source of life! It's less about your own perfection and more about your connection.

Do whatever it takes to stay connected to Jesus. Be refreshed in the freedom that you don't have to be the source for everyone and everything! That's not your role. Allow God to do His role in your life so you can do yours, to His glory!

Read God's Word

Over the next two days, I recommend you read John 15:12-17 and Galatians 5:16-26

#MOMLIFE DEVOTIONAL

Hearing God

• WEEK TWELVE •

Week Twelve

Do You Hear Me?

> "My sheep listen to my voice; I know them, and they follow me."
>
> ***John 10:27 (NLT)***

"Do you hear what I am saying?" That's a question I seem to ask *at least* once a day to my boys. It comes out in many different conversations.

> "We are leaving the park in five minutes to head home. Do you hear me?"
> "As soon as you finish your snack, I want you to get started on your homework. Do you hear me?"
> "Your chores need to be done before you play any electronics. Do you hear me?"
> "Don't talk to your brother like that. Do you hear me?"
> "Make sure all the clothes are picked up off your bedroom floor. Do you hear me?"
> "Stop whining. Do you hear me?"
> "No, you can't have candy for breakfast! Do you hear me?"

What I'm really saying is, "Are you listening? Do you comprehend what I'm explaining to you?" If I don't intentionally give them a moment to acknowledge me, they typically come back with, "But I didn't hear you!" So, to avoid frustration on both our parts, I verify. It would be so wonderful if they'd just listen the first time every time, but we haven't mastered that yet. If we ever do, I won't have to ask, "Do you hear me?" quite so often.

It wasn't always this way. One of the most special moments after giving birth was when each of my sons heard my voice for the first time. All four reacted the same way. As soon as I took each one in my arms and spoke to him, he turned his tiny head towards me—because he knew my voice. Those first few days in the hospital, many people visited, and nurses went in and out. There were many voices talking, but when I spoke, no matter who was there, my child always responded to the sound of my voice.

That blissful stage lasted for a while, but as soon as those babies got mobile, crawling and walking around, there were so many new things to distract them from my voice. From that point on, my voice has had plenty of competition.

Now those four tiny heads are bigger and much louder, and they do not usually turn towards me the first time I speak. But they still *know* my voice. They can pick mine out of a crowd of other mom voices. We have a connection. I know them. They know me.

I want my voice to be an ongoing, familiar presence that they carry with them. Not in a nagging, critical tone, but in a wise, loving way that guides them as they go through life. Distractions may lurk around every corner, but I will continue seeking out their hearts.

In our loud, hectic world, let's never lose our sensitivity to God's voice. As His daughter, I wonder how many times God has had to ask me, "Do you hear what I am saying?" There have been seasons in my life where I have consistently sought out God's voice through Bible reading as well as by praying and listening. Then there have been times when I became busy and neglected those disciplines. What I've learned is this: just like things don't usually work out well when my kids aren't listening to me, the same is true when I'm not intentionally listening to my Heavenly Father.

How I *need* to hear His voice. How I long to be led by it. May my desire (or at least my discipline) always lead me to seek it out.

In His love and grace, He continually reaches out to us, extending the invitation to draw near and listen. May we learn to listen often and listen well. Let's not be the mamas that allow the chaos and busyness of life to dictate what we do and what we listen to. Though distractions may vie for our attention, we can attune our ears to hear Him amid the clamor, sports, homework, friends, birthday parties, family gatherings, and errands.

Just like our children are familiar with our voices, we will get to know God's voice more as we spend time reading His Word and in prayer.

Let's Pray:

Lord, I long to hear You in my everyday life. Help attune my ears to sense when You are speaking to me. Help me to diligently carve out time to spend with You so that Your voice always stays familiar to my spirit. I am so grateful that You are a God who speaks to Your children. In Jesus' Name, Amen.

DAILY REFLECTION

Day 1

"The sheep that are My own hear My voice and listen to Me; I know them, and they follow Me."

John 10:27 (AMP)

1. How often do you listen for God?

2. In what ways has God spoken to you?

3. Take a moment to write about the last time you sensed God speaking to you?

4. What was your response to this? What was the outcome?

5. List two or three ways that you can carve out on a daily basis to spend more time in prayer and Bible reading on a daily basis.

DAILY REFLECTION

Day 2

"My sheep know my voice, and I know them. They follow me"

John 10:27 (CEV)

"Be still, and know that I am God!"

Psalm 46:10 (NLT)

1. In order to hear and know God's voice, we have to quiet the noise around us as well as inside us. In what ways are you able to do this well? Do you struggle with this at all? Explain your answers.

2. List some distractions that keep you from being still before the Lord.

3. Below, list one way that you can either eliminate these distractions or reorganize your time so that you can become an intentional listener to Him.

4. When you are *still* before the Lord, how does it help you to better know that He is God? What does it do for your perspective about your current situations?

5. Spend a few moments now being quiet before the Lord. Write down anything you sense that He is saying to you.

DAILY REFLECTION

Day 3

"My sheep respond to my voice, and I know who they are. They follow me,"

John 10:27 (GW)

Our view of God determines the way we approach Him. Because of that, it is important for us to identify and, in some cases, more accurately clarify our perception of God.

As my relationship with Him really began to grow through prayer and scripture study in my young adult years, I realized that up until that point I had viewed God like He was a cop. I could call on Him if I was in trouble and needed Him. However, I mostly felt like He was just waiting for me to mess up, like a police officer waits on the side of the road with his radar gun in hand. You know that feeling you get in the pit of your stomach when an officer is driving behind you? That's how I usually felt approaching God in prayer. So as my understanding of God's character, based on His Word, matured, I knew I needed a perspective shift – to see God beyond my preconceived fears. My viewpoint wasn't biblical. It was wrong.

We need to keep the right picture of who God is in our minds. It truly affects so much of our relationship with Him.

The Bible tells us the He is the Good Shepherd who cares about His sheep. Psalm 23 tends to be a familiar passage of Scripture. In it, we see the Lord referred to as our Shepherd, leading, guiding, and caring for His flock.

1. Read through it below in the Message translation.

> "God, my shepherd! I don't need a thing. You have bedded me down in lush meadows, you find me quiet pools to drink from. True to your word, you let me catch my breath and send me in the right direction. Even when the way goes through Death Valley, I'm not afraid when you walk at my side. Your trusty shepherd's crook makes me feel secure. You serve me a six-course dinner right in front of my enemies. You revive my drooping head; my cup brims with blessing. Your beauty and love chase after me every day of my life. I'm back home in the house of God for the rest of my life."

2. According to these verses, describe the kind of relationship God wants to have with us.

3. Is this how you currently describe your relationship with God? Explain your answer.

4. How would your daily life change if your perspective of God shifted to a more accurate Biblical viewpoint?

5. Sit for a moment today and allow the Lord to help you "catch your breath." As you direct your focus toward Him, your spirit will be refreshed. If you realize that your view of God has been inaccurate, spend some time praying that God will lead you into truth as you continue to seek Him.

DAILY REFLECTION

Day 4

"My sheep recognize my voice. I know them, and they follow me."

John 10:27 (TM)

1. We hear God's voice when we position ourselves attentively. Do you consistently seek out God's direction? Why or why not?

2. Read John 10:11-16 (NLT).

"I am the good shepherd. The good shepherd sacrifices his life for the sheep. A hired hand will run when he sees a wolf coming. He will abandon the sheep because they don't belong to him and he isn't their shepherd. And so the wolf attacks them and scatters the flock. The hired hand runs away because he's working only for the money and doesn't really care about the sheep.

"I am the good shepherd; I know my own sheep, and they know me, just as my Father knows me and I know the Father. So I sacrifice my life for the sheep. I have other sheep, too, that are not in this sheepfold. I must bring them also. They will listen to my voice, and there will be one flock with one shepherd.

3. Jesus says this phrase twice within these verses, "I am the ___________ _________________."

4. What does this passage tell you about the heart of God towards His followers?

5. Allow those truths to sink in for a few moments today. You are loved and cared for. You were sought out by the Good Shepherd. He desires a close relationship with you. Seek Him! Talk to Him. And then come and listen.

DAILY REFLECTION

Day 5—Wrap Up

"My sheep listen to my voice; I know them, and they follow me."

John 10:27 (NLT)

Hebrews 13:8 says "Jesus Christ is the same yesterday, today, and forever." (NLT)

Throughout Scripture, He has consistently been a God who speaks. He hasn't changed in our day, either. The Lord still speaks. This week's verse states that as His sheep (His followers), we can hear His voice. Just like our kids know our voice, let's train our ears to hear the voice of our Heavenly Father. Let's remind ourselves how much we like it when our kids listen the *first* time! Can we become that kind of listener to God? I believe we can. I'm working on it daily, and I'm praying for your heart to jump on board as well.

If you don't think you've heard God speak to you, or maybe it's been awhile since you have, don't be discouraged! Determine to lean in. Dedicate time to pray and talk to Him about what's on your heart—and then listen. Be intentional about it. Rid yourself of distractions. Ask the Holy Spirit to help you sense what God is speaking to you. As you do, write down what He says. It may be a word, a phrase, a statement, a Scripture verse, or a whole conversation, but whatever it is, write it down.

The more time you spend in prayer, the easier it'll become to pick up on His voice. There is no formula or set of rules. Just make some time, bring your heart, and choose to listen.

Read God's Word

Over the next two days, I recommend you read John 10:1-15 and Isaiah 40:6-11

#MOMLIFE DEVOTIONAL

Thankful Hearts

• **WEEK** THIRTEEN •

Week Thirteen

Oh, Crumb!

"Give thanks in all circumstances, for this is God's will for you in Christ Jesus."

1 Thessalonians 5:18 (NIV)

My kitchen was bright with the morning sunshine gleaming through the window, but the sunny glow did not reflect my mood. I was exhausted yet again from the sleep deprivation that comes from having two kids under the age of two. My oldest son, who was about 18-months-old at the time, was an early riser. On this particular morning, I dragged myself into the kitchen to start making his breakfast. He had requested toast, so I had made him a piece complete with butter and jelly.

I set him up in his little booster chair at our kitchen table, sat down beside him, and he beamed his handsome smile at me as I took his little hands in mine. We closed our eyes and bowed our heads to sing grace.

Yes, you read that right. The nursery workers at our church had taught the kids a song to sing before they ate their snacks in class, and now my son wanted to sing that song before all of our meals at home. Since I'd heard the tune a lot since then, I knew what was coming, but it still never failed to lift my heart. Using the melody of the nursery rhyme *Frère Jacques*, it goes like this:

"Thank You Father, thank You Father / for this food, for this food / and Your many blessings, and Your many blessings / Amen, Amen."

So, we sat together, we sang his song, and he took a bite of his toast. The toast did what toast often does—it shed several crumbs as his little teeth bit off a larger piece. He looked down at those crumbs, then back up at me with a twinkle in his blue eyes, and said repeatedly, "Need pay *dis* toast." It took me hearing him a couple times before I understood that he was actually saying, "Need to pray for *this* toast," pointing at the crumbs that had fallen onto his plate.

It was so precious that, of course, I helped him pray over *those* toast crumbs, too. We sang the song again, bite two happened, and guess what? Yep, more crumbs tumbled down. Do you think those went unnoticed to my observant little guy? Not a chance. He repeated his little statement until we had prayed *again* for *those* crumbs. He had now completed three prayers and two bites of toast. He took a third bite, and the same thing happened!

Did I cook his toast a little too long? Perhaps, but we ended up praying over every crumb that fell off my son's toast. I mean *every* one of them.

By the fifth prayer or so (I honestly lost count), I stopped taking his hands in mine. I also sped up the pace of the song, trying to move things along. *Really?* I thought. *How long is this going to take?* Once I even included the plate and all future crumbs in our prayer, then told him, "We've prayed over your toast, all the crumbs, and even the plate. I think we're good here, buddy." But he would not be deterred from his mission.

Finally, 30 minutes later, he finished that single piece of toast and its billions of crumbs. After I wiped the butter and jelly off his lips and watched him happily patter away into the other room, I walked his plate over to the sink, trying to figure out how in the world I was going to make up for the time I'd just lost with all that praying—and was instantly reminded of our verse for the week.

At that moment, I realized my small son had taught me a big lesson. He was eager to give thanks, repeatedly, for something so trifling as crumbs. Yes, it had probably become a bit of a game for him, but he was adamant about it all the same. He never grew weary in giving thanks. He didn't look at it as a waste of time or insignificant. In fact, I know he found joy in doing it, though I had certainly lost mine in the process.

How many times have I forgotten to give thanks? How many times have I gotten so busy that taking the time to stop and offer thanksgiving to the Giver of all good things in my life seemed like a burden? Are there blessings and gifts going unnoticed in my life? Most likely.

When I'm feeling particularly crabby or impatient, I try to think back to my son, his song, and all those crumbs. When I do, I receive renewed perspective to remember all of the Lord's small blessings in my life, those little gifts that I need to take notice of and thank Him for. There's always something to be grateful for, even in my frustrations. It causes me to examine my heart and shift my focus off my problems, needs, wants, and troubles, and *onto* His goodness, grace, love, and purposes for me.

Let's Pray:

Father, thank You. I don't say that often enough, and I need to say it more. You are a good God. You are a good Father. Thank You for everything that You have done for me; for all that You have given me. I am so grateful for Your love and patience with me even when I forget to be thankful. Holy Spirit, please help me to remember to give thanks each and every day. In Jesus' Name, Amen.

DAILY REFLECTION

Day 1

"Be thankful in all circumstances, for this is God's will for you who belong to Christ Jesus."

1 Thessalonians 5:18 (NLT)

Practice thankfulness today. You don't have to *feel* grateful to express thanks. Sometimes we need to discipline ourselves in order to make thankfulness a way of life, and the best way to do that is to practice.

1. Think about and list three areas of your life that you have taken for granted.

2. Why do you think that has happened?

3. Have your emotions dictated when and how you show gratitude? Explain your answer.

4. Make a list of things that you can give thanks for today. Write it here, in your journal, or type it into your phone. Keep your list handy. My challenge to you this week is to add at least one thing to that list each day.

5. Spend a few moments offering thanks to God and asking the Holy Spirit to help you remember anything you are overlooking as mere "crumbs."

DAILY REFLECTION

Day 2

"Whatever happens, keep thanking God because of Jesus Christ. This is what God wants you to do."

1 Thessalonians 5:18 (CEV)

1. Read Luke 17:11-19 below and underline who showed gratitude.

"As Jesus continued on toward Jerusalem, he reached the border between Galilee and Samaria. As he entered a village there, ten men with leprosy stood at a distance, crying out, 'Jesus, Master, have mercy on us!' He looked at them and said, 'Go show yourselves to the priests.' And as they went, they were cleansed of their leprosy. One of them, when he saw that he was healed, came back to Jesus, shouting, 'Praise God!' He fell to the ground at Jesus' feet, thanking him for what he had done. This man was a Samaritan. Jesus asked, 'Didn't I heal ten men? Where are the other nine? Has no one returned to give glory to God except this foreigner?' And Jesus said to the man, 'Stand up and go. Your faith has healed you.'" (NLT)

2. In the space provided, write down what happened in your own words.

3. Have you ever found yourself taking for granted acts of kindness done by those who are closer to you than those done by a stranger or an acquaintance? Why or why not?

4. Why is it significant that the Samaritan, or in other words, the outsider, was the only one who came back to give thanks?

5. Write down the name of one person in your life who you could show your gratitude to this week? Make an effort to do so in whatever way you are able to (phone call, text, email, gift card, hug), even if it's simply by telling them "thank you."

DAILY REFLECTION

Day 3

"Give thanks no matter what happens. God wants you to thank him because you believe in Christ Jesus."

1 Thessalonians 5:18 (NIRV)

Many times, the things we complain about the most are tied to something we can actually be grateful for. For example, my laundry is never completely done. I may have a load done, but there is always another one right behind it. I do not enjoy doing laundry, but I sure do enjoy all the bodies in my home that are wearing these clothes every day. Most of them call me "Mama," and one calls me "Babe." I'm so thankful that God has blessed me with *each* of them, and I try to remember that when I'm sorting endless piles of socks!

1. Think of two things in your everyday life that frustrate you. What is something to be thankful for in them? List your responses below.

2. According to today's translation of our verse for the week, why is it God's will for us to always have an attitude of gratitude?

3. Do you see a correlation currently in your life between your faith in the Lord and your faithfulness in expressing thanks? If not, how can you start today? Explain your answers below.

4. Take a few moments to write a prayer of thanksgiving to God. Be as specific as possible.

5. Now read your prayer out loud, allowing yourself to meditate on it.

DAILY REFLECTION

Day 4

"Give thanks in everything, for this is the will of God toward you in Christ Jesus."

1 Thessalonians 5:18 (BLB)

1. A funny thing happens when we choose to thank the Lord from our mouth; our eyes start focusing on our blessings rather than on our problems. Below, write about a time when you found this to be true in your own life.

2. Read Psalm 100:

    Shout with joy to the Lord, all the earth!
    Worship the Lord with gladness.
    Come before him, singing with joy.
    Acknowledge that the Lord is God!
    He made us, and we are his.
    We are his people, the sheep of his pasture.
    Enter his gates with thanksgiving;
    go into his courts with praise.
    Give thanks to him and praise his name.
    For the Lord is good.
    His unfailing love continues forever,
    and his faithfulness continues to each generation. (NLT)

3. Today, find some time to be alone with the Lord. Then choose one of the exhortations given to us in Psalm 100 and do it. If you can shout, shout your praise. If you have the ability to sing (even if no one else should hear you but God), sing to the Lord.

4. How does it make you feel to intentionally and verbally express gratefulness?

5. Remind your heart today that He deserves our praise because He is a good, faithful, holy, loving, and very real God. Expressing thankfulness shouldn't depend on how we feel, but it will almost always change how we feel. As you begin to intentionally show gratitude, watch how joy starts to fill you right up.

DAILY REFLECTION

Day 5—Wrap-Up

"Give thanks in all circumstances, for this is God's will for you in Christ Jesus."

1 Thessalonians 5:18 (NIV)

I learned from my 18-month-old son how thankfulness shifts our perspective off ourselves and reminds us of all that we really have. Let's be honest. Some days are just plain hard and the last thing we want to do is discipline ourselves to think about what we are grateful for. I get it. *#MOMLIFE isn't* easy. It's busy, demanding, and often exhausting when our kids are behaving beautifully, let alone when they aren't or other problems arise. However, the Bible is clear that Christ followers are to be thankful because God's goodness truly is all around us. When we take time to recognize that, the heavy load we carry becomes a little bit lighter.

Thankfulness changes our hearts. As we discipline ourselves to cultivate it in our lives, we will reap a beautiful harvest, no matter what we're facing.

One day, those of us who follow Christ will spend eternity praising Him. Let's experience a little bit of Heaven right here on Earth today. Be thankful!

Read God's Word

Over the next two days, I recommend you read Psalm 92:1-15 and Colossians 3:1-4, 12-17

#MOMLIFE DEVOTIONAL

Choose Wisely

• **WEEK** FOURTEEN •

Week Fourteen

So Many Choices

"Today I have given you the choice between life and death, between blessings and curses. Now I call on heaven and earth to witness the choice you make. Oh, that you would choose life, so that you and your descendants might live! You can make this choice by loving the Lord your God, obeying him, and committing yourself firmly to him. This is the key to your life. And if you love and obey the Lord, you will live long in the land the Lord swore to give your ancestors Abraham, Isaac, and Jacob."

Deuteronomy 30:19-20 (NLT)

I talk to my boys quite often about choices. In our home we started teaching them about making choices at a young age. Do you want applesauce or yogurt for snack time? Would you like to wear pants or shorts? Do you want to play outside or inside?

As they are getting older, their dad and I have started communicating the importance their decisions have on their lives. Almost every day, I find myself saying to at least one of my sons, "It doesn't matter what your brother does. It's *your* choice how you act and how you respond to the way someone else acts. If you don't want to get into trouble, make a good choice." In our parenting, we are seeking to teach our kids life lessons through the decisions they make.

One day, after the boys had overloaded on playing electronics, I told them to figure out something else they could do together. It was early spring, the sun was shining, and the weather was nice, so they ended up outside on their big, net-ringed trampoline. They bounced around and soon began a game of basketball using the hoop attached to the trampoline.

All seemed to be going well until our oldest, a structured, bossy first born, started arguing with our second son, an outgoing, carefree kid who doesn't like anything restrictive. One was insistent they play by the rules and keep score; the other just wanted to shoot baskets and have fun. One wanted there to be a winner and a loser; the other didn't care who won or lost.

Frustrated, the oldest threw the ball hard at his brother because he didn't want to play properly. Tired of being told what to do, my second son retaliated by punching his brother in the face. Both came inside crying. One with a bloody nose.

I cleaned up the injury, sent both boys to their rooms, and later we had a family powwow about choices. "I understand why you were angry," I told the second son, "but that doesn't give you an excuse to punch your brother in the face. That was a bad choice." Then I looked at the oldest. "And I get why you were upset, but that doesn't excuse you from throwing the ball at him like he was a dodgeball target. That was a bad choice, too."

Then I tried to hammer my message home. "We can't control somebody else's choices. We might get mad or frustrated at their choices, but we are responsible for our own actions. You can't just react. You choose your words and actions." I'm not sure how much of my motivational talk was absorbed into their hearts that day, but I'll continue saying those things day after day, year after year, teaching and training them. What they *did* pick up on was the consequences that ensued from their behavior. Choices do have consequences. That's why our decisions matter so much.

Our Heavenly Father has lined out choices for us, too. In this week's passage, God told the Israelites that He gave them the choice between life and death, blessings and curses—and they had to decide each day which one to choose.

In the midst of the chaos of raising kids, God asks us to make the same daily choice as well. It seems like a no brainer; of course, we all want blessings. But I know I've lost my cool more times with my boys than I'd like to admit. I've spoken in an impatient, annoyed tone. I've snapped at them when stressed out, and I've seen their faces crumple at my reactions. I do not *automatically* choose "life and blessings."

I decided to print out this verse and stick it on the wall of my bedroom so that I could see it every day and be reminded that I have a choice. I get to choose my reactions to motherhood, my husband, my workload—all of it. I decide how I speak, how I spend my time, where I devote my attention, and how I give or withhold love, compliments, and nurturing. As moms, we have the ability to speak life into those around us. Our choices can be building blocks to make them stronger, or a barrier to erect walls between us and our loved ones.

I am so thankful that God's mercies are new every morning (Lamentations 3:23). If yesterday wasn't a "life and blessings" kind of day, make some changes—and the next time chaos reigns, choose well again. Your decisions, even the small ones, matter in big ways.

Let's Pray:

Lord, thank You for the life-giving power that You offer me daily through the Holy Spirit. Help me to remember that my choices matter. When I'm feeling stressed or tired or downcast, help me grab the blessing of peace You offer and choose to walk in it. I want my family to live in Your blessings, and I know that comes from continually choosing Your ways every day. With Your help, I choose life. In Jesus' Name, Amen.

DAILY REFLECTION

Day 1

"I call heaven and earth to witness against you today, that I have set before you life and death, blessing and curse. Therefore choose life, that you and your offspring may live, loving the Lord your God, obeying his voice and holding fast to him, for he is your life and length of days, that you may dwell in the land that the Lord swore to your fathers, to Abraham, to Isaac, and to Jacob, to give them."

Deuteronomy 30:19-20 (ESV)

1. In the above verses, circle the words "choose life."

2. When was the last time you stopped to consider the impact your, daily choices are having on yourself and your family? Take a minute to do so now.

3. Do you like the results? Why or why not?

4. Do your current actions speak of life and blessings? Explain.

5. What can you do today to "choose life?"

DAILY REFLECTION

Day 2

"I call heaven and earth as witnesses against you today, that I have set before you life and death, the blessing and the curse; therefore, you shall choose life in order that you may live, you and your descendants, by loving the Lord your God, by obeying His voice, and by holding closely to Him; for He is your life [your good life, your abundant life, your fulfillment] and the length of your days, that you may live in the land which the Lord promised (swore) to give to your fathers, to Abraham, Isaac, and Jacob."

Deuteronomy 30:19-20 (AMP)

Verse 20 shows how we can choose life and live in God's blessings. In our time of reflection today, let's focus on the method God gives to help us live this out.

1. Write down the three things verse 20 says you need to do to choose life.

2. Do your daily choices reflect these directives? Explain.

3. The verse goes on to say that God is *our life*. Write down the three descriptions of that life listed in the parenthesis within the passage.

4. In your own words, and according to our weekly passage, write down how you can choose the kind of life that our Heavenly Father desires for us.

5. What encouragement do you glean from this passage of scripture?

DAILY REFLECTION

Day 3

"I call Heaven and Earth to witness against you today: I place before you Life and Death, Blessing and Curse. Choose life so that you and your children will live. And love God, your God, listening obediently to him, firmly embracing him. Oh yes, he is life itself, a long life settled on the soil that God, your God, promised to give your ancestors, Abraham, Isaac, and Jacob."

Deuteronomy 30:19-20 (TM)

Let's start a few verses earlier in Deuteronomy 30 and read what comes prior to this week's passage.

"Now listen! Today I am giving you a choice between life and death, between prosperity and disaster. For I command you this day to love the Lord your God and to keep his commands, decrees, and regulations by walking in his ways. If you do this, you will live and multiply, and the Lord your God will bless you and the land you are about to enter and occupy.

But if your heart turns away and you refuse to listen, and if you are drawn away to serve and worship other gods, then I warn you now that you will certainly be destroyed. You will not live a long, good life in the land you are crossing the Jordan to occupy.

Deuteronomy 30:15-18 (NLT)

Progressive growth in spiritual maturity comes as we first set our priorities and then line up our lives (and schedules) accordingly. We often live this out in reverse. If our schedules are not a reflection of what really matters to us, then we are most likely living in reactive mode as opposed to being proactive.

What are your priorities? More importantly, what is your top priority? This passage of scripture clearly talks about keeping God in the number one spot in our hearts. This means prioritizing Him into our daily schedules as busy moms because that doesn't just happen by itself. God directs us to be intentional about making Him our most sought-after pursuit—not just when it is convenient or when we have extra time, but *all* the time.

Reflect honestly on your schedule choices and actions. Do they reveal God in the number one seat of your heart or is there something else there? One of the things I've noticed becoming a trend is families filling their lives so full of activities for the kids that they have little time for anything else. Activities are not necessarily bad, but if there is no margin left, your priorities may need to be adjusted. If raising children with a strong spiritual foundation is important to you, set your schedule accordingly to allow time for spiritual truths to be instilled.

Sometimes getting organized enough to set priorities and follow through with them seems like too much to take on. But something *is* going to set your schedule. It'll either be your priorities or the push and pull of everyday activity and stress—and just like our weekly passage emphasizes, *you* are the one who makes this choice.

Again, God isn't merely suggesting that we put Him first at our earliest convenience. His stance on this matter is sure and unchanging and it is with our best interests at heart. There simply is no better life than the one found in Christ.

1. What is your top priority?

2. As you reflect on the things that make up your life in your regular schedule, are your priorities setting the pace?

3. If you realize God does not occupy first place in your heart, how can you rearrange your priorities so that God has His rightful place, enabling you to live in His blessings?

4. What are four priorities that you either already have in place for your family or that you want to set in place? You may need to discuss this with your spouse before writing down your answer.

Pray about this and challenge yourself to line up your priorities according to God's Word. Then line up your daily and weekly agenda to reflect these priorities.

5. Spend a few moments reflecting on today's verses from Deuteronomy and remind yourself of the promises that God fulfills when you put Him first in your life.

DAILY REFLECTION

Day 4

"Today I ask heaven and earth to be witnesses. I am offering you life or death, blessings or curses. Now, choose life! Then you and your children may live. Love the Lord your God. Obey him. Stay close to him. He is your life. And he will let you live many years in the land. This is the land he promised to give your ancestors Abraham, Isaac and Jacob."

Deuteronomy 30:19-20 (ICB)

In this week's devotional, I referenced Lamentations 3:22-23. It says:

"The faithful love of the Lord never ends! His mercies never cease. Great is his faithfulness; his mercies begin afresh each morning." (NLT)

1. Fill in the blanks from the verses above: The faithful love of the Lord __________ _______! His mercies ______________ _____________ . ___________ is His faithfulness; His mercies begin afresh ___________ morning.

2. It's such a wonderful truth that His mercies "begin afresh each morning." What are five words that come to mind about this passage?

If you're anything like me, *thankful* was one of them. I'll be the first to admit that I really need new mercies each day. I don't want the leftovers, mainly because I've probably used them all up. Our God is so good and so gracious. He knows how to love us well.

3. How do these verses in Lamentations encourage us to keep pressing forward toward the call to choose life that we find in Deuteronomy 30?

4. Praying the Word of God is powerful! If that's not something you're in the practice of doing, I encourage you to start. Let's turn these verses into a prayer of thanksgiving today:

> Father, thank You that Your love is faithful and never ends. I'm so grateful that Your mercies never cease. Great is Your faithfulness! Praise You, Lord, that Your mercies begin afresh each morning. I so need them today.

Soak that in for a moment!

5. Today is a new day and you have the choice as to how you will live it out. Think about a few ways your kids could see you choosing life on a regular basis. Write down your ideas below.

DAILY REFLECTION

Day 5—Wrap-Up

"Today I have given you the choice between life and death, between blessings and curses. Now I call on heaven and earth to witness the choice you make. Oh, that you would choose life, so that you and your descendants might live! You can make this choice by loving the Lord your God, obeying him, and committing yourself firmly to him. This is the key to your life. And if you love and obey the Lord, you will live long in the land the Lord swore to give your ancestors Abraham, Isaac, and Jacob."

Deuteronomy 30:19-20 (NLT)

As we wrap up our study of this week's passage, let me encourage you that no matter how hard it may seem, make the perspective shifts you've discovered this week. When God is your top priority, everything else has a way of falling into place because we sense His leading and direction.

I'm right there with you in doing these "heart inspections" gauging where I'm at and adjusting accordingly. Remember, living a life of God's blessings is a choice that He gives to us. Do we want it? Are we willing to follow His ways?

We are on this journey every day. If we don't like where we're at, we have the freedom to begin doing things differently. As moms, we know the power of choices. When our kids look at us, may they consistently see *us* choosing life!

Read God's Word

Over the next two days, I recommend you read Matthew 6:30-34 and Matthew 7:24-29

#MOMLIFE DEVOTIONAL

Focus

• WEEK FIFTEEN •

Week Fifteen

Three Little Words

"Therefore, since we are surrounded by such a great cloud of witnesses, let us throw off everything that hinders and the sin that so easily entangles. And let us run with perseverance the race marked out for us, fixing our eyes on Jesus, the pioneer and perfecter of faith. For the joy set before him he endured the cross, scorning its shame, and sat down at the right hand of the throne of God. Consider him who endured such opposition from sinners, so that you will not grow weary and lose heart."

Hebrews 12:1-3 (NIV)

In the days that followed the revelation of my mom's cancer diagnosis, every aspect of my normal life changed. I still had a lot of normal things to do—but my emotions were maxed out, my patience was on thin ice, and my attempts to multitask left loose ends that fell through the cracks. I felt pulled in so many directions, I couldn't seem to muster up the energy to do the things I wanted to get done. Frustrated and frazzled, I drifted to anything and everything that could get my attention off the heaviness the diagnosis had brought to my heart and mind.

I scrolled through social media way more than usual and allowed my thoughts to wander aimlessly. I wanted to see what other people were doing in their lives so that I could momentarily escape my own reality. I got distracted in my conversations, literally losing my train of thought mid-sentence. Repeatedly, I'd say, "I'm so sorry. What were we just talking about?" I was distracted in my daily activities, unable to focus on any one thing. The distraction even invaded my prayers. I was all over the place.

I didn't drift intentionally. I *wanted* to focus, to play with my kids, to clean my house, to do something normal. But I couldn't. I was obviously overwhelmed, and in my attempts to overcome I just tried harder and pushed myself more. I *knew* better! I understood that way of living never works. Yet I couldn't break out of the distraction cycle.

A familiar story in the Bible depicts Peter, one of Jesus's disciples, stepping out of a boat on a storm-tossed Sea of Galilee and beginning to walk on the water towards the Lord. Peter was doing something incredible! He knew Jesus. He had personally watched Him do miracles and change impossible circumstances, and here he was, walking on top of the churning waves. Crazy! It didn't take long though for the reality of his stormy surroundings to overwhelm him to the point that He took his eyes off Jesus. "But when he saw the strong wind and the waves, he was terrified and began to sink." (Matthew 14:30, NLT)

I realized the same thing was happening to me as I watched my mom's appetite wane to the point of just a few bites at every meal; as I fed her and helped her stand, walk, use the bathroom, and get dressed; as I sat beside her when she was in so much pain and tried (unsuccessfully) not to cry when the medications sometimes made her forget who I was.

I did not doubt God's existence. I had already dealt with that years earlier as a child when my dad committed suicide. I had wrestled with my faith for years and come to the conclusion with every fiber of my being that God was real. But in that horrific season with my mother I was overwhelmed by the devastation of the circumstances. The heaviness was too much. No matter what the distraction,

I couldn't get out of it—until I chose to fix my eyes on Jesus. Only He could help me rise above the waves that were threatening to pull me under.

Three little words inspired by this week's passage—fix your eyes—echoed in my spirit. They encouraged me to see beyond my physical sight and allow my spiritual vision to guide me to the safety of His loving arms.

When we forget to fix our eyes on Him, we'll get terrified, frustrated, and distracted. We'll sink into despair, loneliness, grief, and anger. Yet when we fix our eyes on God, He really does fix things. It may be our circumstances that are mended, or it may simply be our hearts—but healing is brought, and things *do* change.

This week remember the three little words that'll place your focus on the One who knows how to get you through whatever it is you're going through.

Let's Pray:

God, there are so many things that vie for my attention and focus. Help make me aware of the distractions surrounding me. When I begin to falter and get off course, remind me to readjust my gaze back to You. I need You to be the focal point so that I don't get dizzy spinning through all the demands of life. Thank You that You have given me the way to press through and keep going without getting worn out. I choose to fix my eyes on You today, God. I will look to You as my example, my strength, my focus, my Savior, and my ever-present help. In Jesus' Name, Amen.

DAILY REFLECTION

Day 1

"Therefore, since we have so great a cloud of witnesses surrounding us, let us also lay aside every encumbrance and the sin which so easily entangles us, and let us run with endurance the race that is set before us, fixing our eyes on Jesus, the author and perfecter of faith, who for the joy set before Him endured the cross, despising the shame, and has sat down at the right hand of the throne of God. For consider Him who has endured such hostility by sinners against Himself, so that you will not grow weary and lose heart."

Hebrews 12:1-3 (NASB)

1. Verse 1 tells us to run our race with endurance and to lay aside all distractions and sins that trip us up. How well do you feel like you are doing this right now? Explain your answer.

2. List some of the distractions and/or sins that are currently hindering you as you are running your race.

3. Verse 3 ends by encouraging us to not grow weary and lose heart. When was the last time you felt weary—the kind of weary that weighs down on your soul? What caused it?

4. How do you run with perseverance day in and day out without growing weary? The answer is found right in the middle of our passage. See our three little words in verse 2? Write down those words now.

5. Describe what it would look like for you to daily fix your eyes on Jesus.

DAILY REFLECTION

Day 2

"Therefore, since we are surrounded by such a huge crowd of witnesses to the life of faith, let us strip off every weight that slows us down, especially the sin that so easily trips us up. And let us run with endurance the race God has set before us. We do this by keeping our eyes on Jesus, the champion who initiates and perfects our faith. Because of the joy awaiting him, he endured the cross, disregarding its shame. Now he is seated in the place of honor beside God's throne. Think of all the hostility he endured from sinful people; then you won't become weary and give up."

Hebrews 12:1-3 (NLT)

I closed out this week's devotional by stating that when we fix our eyes on God, He really does fix things.

1. Think about that statement in light of your life. I'm sure you may have encountered situations where that doesn't seem accurate, but let's reflect on that challenging truth from our weekly passage.

2. When you focus on God—especially as you consider all that Hebrews tells you Christ endured—are you encouraged to press on through your own struggles? Why or why not?

Here are two examples of what can happen when we fix our eyes on Jesus. Place a check mark in the box by the ones you've found to be true in your life.

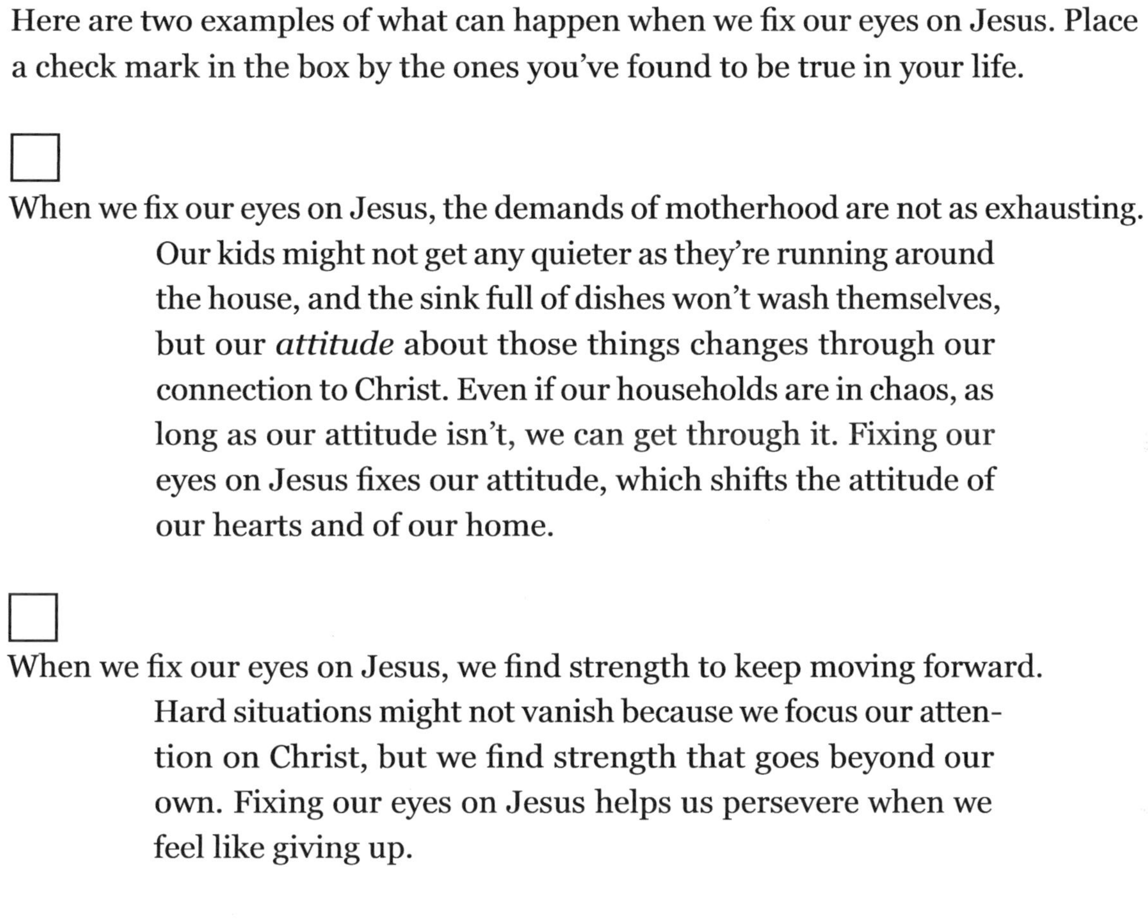

☐

When we fix our eyes on Jesus, the demands of motherhood are not as exhausting.

Our kids might not get any quieter as they're running around the house, and the sink full of dishes won't wash themselves, but our *attitude* about those things changes through our connection to Christ. Even if our households are in chaos, as long as our attitude isn't, we can get through it. Fixing our eyes on Jesus fixes our attitude, which shifts the attitude of our hearts and of our home.

☐

When we fix our eyes on Jesus, we find strength to keep moving forward.

Hard situations might not vanish because we focus our attention on Christ, but we find strength that goes beyond our own. Fixing our eyes on Jesus helps us persevere when we feel like giving up.

Use the space below to write your own statement explaining how you've seen God intervene when you have chosen to fix your eyes on Him.

DAILY REFLECTION

Day 3

"Do you see what this means—all these pioneers who blazed the way, all these veterans cheering us on? It means we'd better get on with it. Strip down, start running—and never quit! No extra spiritual fat, no parasitic sins. Keep your eyes on Jesus, who both began and finished this race we're in. Study how he did it. Because he never lost sight of where he was headed—that exhilarating finish in and with God—he could put up with anything along the way: Cross, shame, whatever. And now he's there, in the place of honor, right alongside God. When you find yourselves flagging in your faith, go over that story again, item by item, that long litany of hostility he plowed through. That will shoot adrenaline into your souls!"

Hebrews 12:1-3 (TM)

Maybe the season you're walking through right now isn't as heavy as the one I shared about this week. Perhaps it's heavier. While I don't know the circumstances surrounding you, I do know we can all use the reminder to fix our eyes on Jesus.

In John Maxwell's book, *The 21 Indispensable Qualities of a Leader*, he tells how experienced animal trainers take a stool with them when they step into a cage with a lion. Why a stool? When the trainer holds the stool with the legs extended toward the lion's face, the animal tries to focus on all four legs at once—and that paralyzes him. Maxwell concluded, "Divided focus always works against you."

What we focus on directs our lives. I'm sure we can all think of times we've become paralyzed by fear, worry, obstacles, or the sheer volume of things happening at any given moment on this motherhood journey. If we want to stay the course and do this *#MOMLIFE* well, we must continually redirect our attention to where it should be—Christ. We do this through prayer, scripture reading, and biblical teaching. These things help to refocus our vision. They steady our line of sight in the midst of chaos, distraction, and confusion.

Because our focus is vital to our success and fulfillment in life, God directs us to set it on the only constant we will find this side of Heaven: Him.

1. List two or three examples where you've seen yourself become paralyzed when your focus has been on too many things at once?

2. What repercussions does that have on your daily mothering?

3. Circle the answer below that best describes how often you need the reminder to *fix your eyes on Jesus*?

    - Somewhat Often
    - Daily

- Several times a day
- Rarely
- I don't need the reminder

4. If you circled any of the first four options above, write down some practical ways that you can help yourself stay more mindful of this God-given directive?

5. Write out this week's passage, Hebrews 12:1-3, in your favorite translation.

DAILY REFLECTION

Day 4

"Therefore we also, since we are surrounded by so great a cloud of witnesses, let us lay aside every weight, and the sin which so easily ensnares us, and let us run with endurance the race that is set before us, looking unto Jesus, the author and finisher of our faith, who for the joy that was set before Him endured the cross, despising the shame, and has sat down at the right hand of the throne of God. For consider Him who endured such hostility from sinners against Himself, lest you become weary and discouraged in your souls."

Hebrews 12:1-3 (NKJV)

1. Look at Hebrews 12:2 and fill in the blanks: "Looking unto Jesus, the __________ and _________ of our faith, who for the joy that was set before Him endured the cross, despising the shame, and has sat down at the right hand of the throne of God."

2. Explain what it means to you that Christ is the author and finisher of your faith.

3. Has your faith given you boldness to step out and do something that, without it, would be scary or seem ridiculous? Explain your answer.

4. When Peter took his eyes off Jesus in Matthew 14, he began to sink. Can you think of a time when your focus wandered, and in your distraction, you found yourself sinking into despair?

5. Today, encourage yourself in your faith. Peter felt bold because his eyes were on Jesus. We can experience that same boldness in our lives and in our circumstances. We can step out instead of shrinking back. We can trust instead of giving in to fear, and we can teach our children to do the same.

DAILY REFLECTION

Day 5—Wrap-Up

"Therefore, since we are surrounded by such a great cloud of witnesses, let us throw off everything that hinders and the sin that so easily entangles. And let us run with perseverance the race marked out for us, fixing our eyes on Jesus, the pioneer and perfecter of faith. For the joy set before him he endured the cross, scorning its shame, and sat down at the right hand of the throne of God. Consider him who endured such opposition from sinners, so that you will not grow weary and lose heart."

Hebrews 12:1-3 (NIV)

We never find the answer by keeping our eyes on the problem. We need to look up.

I find it interesting how many directives are given to us in this passage:

- Let us throw off
- Let us run with perseverance
- Fix our eyes on Jesus
- Consider Him

These are things Paul tells us to do. He's not saying to pray and ask God if He wants us to do these things. Paul exhorts, "Do them!" Will we discipline ourselves accordingly? Let's decide together to stay proactive in this journey of faith. Each day let's purposefully fix our gaze on Christ so that we can run our race without becoming exhausted moms and deflated women.

Remember, Jesus is perfecting you day by day as you look to Him in trust.

Read God's Word

Over the next two days, I recommend you read Matthew 14:22-33 and 2 Timothy 4:1-8.

#MOMLIFE DEVOTIONAL

Intentional Living

• WEEK SIXTEEN •

Week Sixteen

Be Where Your Feet Are

"This is the day that the Lord has made. Let us rejoice and be glad today!"

Psalm 118:24 (NCV)

Several years ago, a very wise "spiritual mama" gave me some of the best advice I've ever heard. She was a leader in our women's ministry, and it was as though she always went out of her way to encourage me. She was a grandma, had a heart for young moms, and often came up to me offering a big hug and asking how I was doing.

On this particular Sunday, she found me after church was over as I was picking up my kids from the nursery. In her calm, peaceful manner she must've sensed I was especially frazzled and tired after another morning of ministry alongside my husband with my toddler and baby in tow.

She released me from her embrace, then said, "Alison, you just need to be where your feet are." The phrase grabbed my attention, and as she then went on to explain what it meant, I felt refreshed and empowered.

"Be where your feet are" is all about showing up intentionally each day in the season of life you currently find yourself. Too often we disconnect from our life as we are living it. Many times, we jump ahead planning for the next season, thinking that things will be much better when we can just get to that next phase of life. "When I find the right guy, I'll enjoy my life!" "When I get married, I'll be happy." "When

I can afford a better home, I'll feel satisfied." "When I can set aside more money in savings, I'll stop worrying so much." "When I have kids, life will be exciting." "When my kids get a little older, I can have time for friendships again." "When my kids aren't so busy with various activities, I'll be able to do some of the things I'd like to do."

Sometimes we disconnect from the present reality simply from all our multitasking. For me, I often find myself home with my kids while answering phone calls, responding to emails, scrolling through social media, planning the week, and trying (usually unsuccessfully) to clean my house or catch up on laundry—all at the same time.

Yet in all that *doing*, I'm missing the *being*. Even more, I'm missing the peace that should come with the *being* because I can't enjoy it or rest in it when I'm driving myself, and everyone else, crazy with all the *doing*.

Now, I know we can't just sit on the floor all day playing with our kids. Other things need to get done. However, when we spend the majority of our time multitasking, we are never truly focusing on any one thing. How often do our families really get our *full* attention? If we're honest, trying to get ten things done at once results in frustration anyway!

Choosing to be where our feet are causes us to give our total, undivided attention to the moment and to the people we're with in that moment. In a society filled with distraction, we have to *fight* for authentic connection. We have to fully engage. Instead of operating in autopilot mode, let's take the controls and open our eyes and our hearts to what is going on *right now*.

I've also learned that I can't be where my feet are when I'm too busy trying to be where someone else's feet are. Comparison between moms is a real thing, and it damages our emotional and spiritual health. Comparison causes us to miss the beauty of the moments that are happening all around us. It causes us to look through eyes of contempt at some of the very things with which God has blessed us. When we try so hard to keep up and catch up with others, we can't enjoy what's right under our own feet. As moms, we can certainly learn from each other, but let's not get stuck comparing our lives, looks, families, husbands, incomes, homes, kids, clothing, vacations, and so on, to anyone else's. Instead, be where *your* feet are—and do it with a thankful heart for what you already have.

Finally, I encourage you to "be where your feet are" even when it's difficult. It may seem counterintuitive to want to be *in the moment* when we are experiencing transition, loss, grief, heartache, or change. Why should we want to fully embrace the sleep deprivation that comes with a newborn, the patience required for toddlers or teenagers, or the changes of menopause?

When you allow yourself to be present in these times, you'll be more likely to pick up on God's insights for you in those circumstances and more able to sense His love manifested to you and your family amid your trials. Seasons come and go, so don't miss out on today just because you can't wait to get it over with and move on.

Right now, I'm reminding myself that my current noisy, chaotic, non-stop season of life won't last forever. The next season will have its own concerns, but as long as I'm in this one, I want to fully experience it, enjoy it, and soak up every blessing and lesson to be learned.

This day is filled with opportunities to live intentionally. My hope and prayer is that we will recognize them and be where our feet are!

Let's Pray:

Father, Your Word reminds me to focus on today. It's so easy to think ahead, but in doing that, I'm missing out. Thank You for the season of life I'm living right now. It has its challenges, but You have promised to never leave me, so I know You will help me through. Lead me, Lord. Help me to navigate today well so that I can live intentionally. The days are usually hard and I'm often tired, but Your mercies are new every morning. Help me learn to say "no" to distraction and "yes" to relationship. This is the day that You have made, so I will choose joy as I live it out. In Jesus' Name, Amen.

DAILY REFLECTION

Day 1

"This is the day the Lord has made. We will rejoice and be glad in it."

Psalm 118:24 (NLT)

1. This week, we are talking about showing up more and being present in the moment. How well do you feel you are doing this now?

2. Do you often find yourself multitasking? In what ways?

3. List what happens to your own emotional state, as well as that of your kids and those around you, when you multitask with them present.

4. What feelings or thoughts usually pop up as you start your mornings?

For me, stress, worry, and fear have all been feelings I've encountered at the start of the day as a mom. I've realized, though, that I experience those feelings when I'm not being present. Worry propels us into the future and causes us to chase around "what ifs." When I choose to trust that God will help me with all that I'll encounter *today,* I can be content where my feet are, and my stress level gets under control.

5. How can being where your feet are help you better manage your emotions?

DAILY REFLECTION

Day 2

"This is the day which the Lord hath made; we will rejoice and be glad in it."

Psalm 118:24 (KJV)

1. Describe what your current season of life looks like right now.

2. How can *being where your feet are* help you personally become more intentional with your moments? With your family? With yourself? With your time?

3. Below, write down the statement, "Be where your feet are."

4. What are some ways that you can accomplish this today?

5. Spend a few moments praying about your day today. Share with God about the challenges you are facing and ask for His help. Take a moment to thank Him for this day and all it holds.

Starting the day intentionally connecting with God will help you live with more purpose as you move forward into your day.

DAILY REFLECTION

Day 3

"This [day in which God has saved me] is the day which the Lord has made; Let us rejoice and be glad in it."

Psalm 118:24 (AMP)

Because I'm a mom of four kids who works in ministry and writes whenever I can, I am regularly asked, "How do you do it all?"

I used to freeze up whenever that question came my way. For some reason, I usually sensed an undertone of judgment with it, as though people were either assuming I was overextending myself or that I was somehow able to carry a big load in ways they weren't. Whether that judgment was real or just a result of my overthinking brain, I don't know, but it left me feeling self-defensive, frustrated, and needing to downplay my accomplishments.

Ironically, though, I also looked at other moms who homeschooled, blogged, ran a business, and kept beautifully decorated homes and thought, *How in the world do they do it?* I'd ask the question, but avoid answering it myself.

After spending time in prayer and reflection about this, I found God's take on it in His Word. One of the key things to "being where your feet are" is learning how to live with what I like to call a *grace pace*. In Matthew 11:28-30 from The Message, Jesus teaches us:

"Are you tired? Worn out? Burned out on religion? Come to me. Get away with me and you'll recover your life. I'll

> show you how to take a real rest. Walk with me and work with me—watch how I do it. Learn the unforced rhythms of grace. I won't lay anything heavy or ill-fitting on you. Keep company with me and you'll learn to live freely and lightly."

We can live our daily lives *in rhythm with Jesus*. It's a rhythm that frees us from the entanglement of unnecessary distractions and burdens that trip us up and wear us out. It's a rhythm that helps us accomplish all that God has purposed us to do—and as long as we walk in this grace pace, we won't burn out doing it!

We will avoid unwanted stress by simply choosing to stay in step with Jesus instead of trying to run ahead or getting worked up about all the things we can't control right now. That's what a grace pace is all about. God gives us the grace for what we are facing *today*—and He'll do it again tomorrow and the day after that.

Being where our feet are as we walk in His grace allows us to be effective, not just busy.

1. Does the daily rhythm of your life currently reflect a 'grace pace?" Why or why not?

2. There are three questions asked right at in the beginning of Matthew 11:28 in The Message translation. Write them below, circling the one(s) that speaks to you the most.

3. Following those questions, Jesus begins to line out how we recover our lives, learn to really rest, and live freely and lightly. He directs us to:

    a. Come to Him
    b. Get away with Him
    c. Walk with Him
    d. Work with Him
    e. Watch how He does it
    f. Learn the unforced rhythms of grace
    g. Keep company with Him

All of these are action steps on our part, but they speak less of following rules and more of accepting an invitation. From this passage, summarize Jesus's goal of asking us to draw closer to Him.

4. Revisit the seven invitations listed in the previous question. Beside each one, write a practical way that you can implement that directive into your life.

5. Think about and explain how being where your feet are can encourage you to live at a grace pace.

DAILY REFLECTION

Day 4

"This is the day which the Lord has made; Let us rejoice and be glad in it."

Psalm 118:24 (NASB)

1. Have you been more intentional this week? How? With who? What have been the outcomes?

At the end of our devotion for this week, I mentioned how comparison can make it hard for us to enjoy where our feet are at on our journey. I don't struggle with its pull as much as I used to, but if I'm honest, I'm still tempted at times to base my worth off of what someone else is doing. Social media has given us unprecedented access to the personal lives of others. At any moment we can pull up hundreds of pictures to see what others are wearing, where they are going out to eat, and where they went on vacation—and it's easy to start believing our lives just don't measure up.

Comparison isn't something that ends after high school. It's very much a part of our *#MOMLIFE.* But when we compare, we aren't being where our feet are. We're running around trying to be where someone else's feet are, and therefore distracted from what God has already provided for us and destined for our future.

2. When was the last time you compared yourself to someone else? Write about it below.

3. In what ways has comparison robbed you?

4. What safeguards can you put in your life to help you not fall prey to the dangerous pull of comparison?

5. From our weekly verse, the word "rejoice" speaks of joy and excitement. When was the last time you felt excited about your day? Write about it below.

Spend some time thanking God for *your* journey, *your* life, *your* kids, and *your* blessings. Ask Him to help you see what's right under your own feet so you can rejoice today in His love and provision for you.

DAILY REFLECTION

Day 5—Wrap-Up

"This is the day that the Lord has made. Let us rejoice and be glad today!"

Psalm 118:24 (NCV)

Show up for yourself! Show up for other people in your life. Let's fight for our relationships and not be sidelined by distraction. Let's be present, rooted right where we are.

Each person, small and big, that call us "mom" are a gift from God! How we speak to them and treat them matters! Busy schedules can cause us to simply live alongside each other in the same household, with little or no real connection, but that doesn't have to be our story. Lean in, mamas. Start conversations. Continue conversations. Fight for their hearts. Share your heart. Choose joy. This is the day the Lord has made! How we live it is up to us.

My prayer for us is that we will decide to be where our feet are as we live connected, intentional, and filled with love, joy, and grace.

Read God's Word

Over the next two days, I recommend you read Psalms 84:1-12 and Psalms 118:19-29.

#MOMLIFE DEVOTIONAL

You've Got This

#MOMLIFE Wrap-Up

I pray that you have been encouraged, challenged, and filled with hope these past sixteen weeks. Motherhood isn't easy. We need encouragement. We need constant reminders to breathe and lean into God's grace in the middle of the messes, attitudes, tough decisions, and the daily pull of consistent parenting. He's entrusted us with the role of shaping hearts and lives. And thankfully, He hasn't left us alone to do it!

If we'll simply take the time to come to God in prayer each day, He'll equip us for the task at hand. Don't give up, mama! Keep pursuing your child's heart. Keep knocking on their door. Keep asking questions. Continue validating and affirming them. Continue training them in truth and love. Communicate and over communicate your affection for them.

Stay in God's Word often and be encouraged that He's got you! And because He does, you can live your *#MOMLIFE* with wisdom, joy, peace, and hope.

Connect with Alison

Check out Alison's other book

"**Living Freedom: Losing a Spiritaul 10lbs**" and learn how to let go of baggage and live a life of true freedom.

55642552R00146

Made in the USA
San Bernardino,
CA